THE QUEEN MOTHER – *HER LIFE STORY*

Contents

Thank Heaven for Little Girls!

The day that changed Her life

War and Peace!

Bowing to a New Sovereign

The Autumn of Her days

PUBLISHER'S NOTE: Due to their age, the condition of some early pictures used in this book is not of as high a standard as the publisher would wish to maintain. The decision was made, however, that to omit these historical pictures would greatly affect the value of this book as a pictorial record, and they were therefore included, despite their reproductive quality.

PICTURE ACKNOWLEDGEMENTS

BBC Hulton Picture Library	82. 84–85. 86–87. 108–109. 110–111. 136–137. 138–139. 142–143. 144. 197. 207 (top). 232–233. 252–253. 272–273. 274–275.
Camera Press	Front and Back Covers. 36. 42–43 (top). 62–63. 66–67. 69 (top). 72–73. 78. 79–83. 96–97. 98. 104–105. 106–107. 112–113. 128–129. 140–141. 177. 178–179. 180–181. 184–185. 186–187. 188–189. 190–191. 196. 205. 206–207 (bottom). 210–211. 218. 222–223. 246–247. 248–249. 250–251. 252–253. 254–255. 256–257. 258–259. 261. 262–263. 264–265. 266–267. 268–269. 270–271. 276–277. 278–279. 280–281.
Country Life Books	212–213. 214–215. 216–217.
Paul Cullen Collection	39. 43 (bottom). 44. 50–51. 52–53. 54 (top). 58–59. 61. 64. 68. 74–75. 76–77. 81. 99. 102–103.
Imperial War Museum	114–115. 120–121 (top). 130–131.
J McDonald	219. 220–221. 224–225. 226–227. 228–229.
Photographers International	236–237. 238–239. 240–241. 242–243. 260. 282–283. 284–285.
The Photo Source	74. 122–123. 124–125. 182–183. 198. 202–203. 208.
Popperphoto	70–71. 90–91. 94–95. 126–127. 192. 193. 194–195. 209.
Press Association	48–49.
Rex Features	234–235.
Royal Archives, Windsor	56–57. 65. 69 (bottom). 80. 100–101. 121.
Syndication International	33. 34–35. 37–38. 40–41. 45. 46–47. 54 (bottom)–55. 60. 75. 88–89. 92. 93. 116–117. 118–119. 134–135. 199. 200–201. 204. 230–231. 244–245.

SHE IS AS OLD as the century. It is more than three decades since she shared the British Throne with her late husband, yet she is still so universally admired that children dashed forward to present her with flowers and gifts on her 86th birthday this year; such is the love everyone seems to have for Her Majesty Queen Elizabeth, The Queen Mother, a woman who never wanted to be near the centre of the world stage, but someone who has often been touched by and has herself touched the history of the Twentieth Century.

THE QUEEN MOTHER — HER LIFE STORY, covers her fascinating journey from childhood up to the present time, when she has become affectionately known as "everybody's grandma." The book not only deals with her own biography, but through that special role she has always had, give us insights into the history of our time. It is lavishly illustrated with more than 200 photographs, both colour and black and white.

Elizabeth Angela Marguerite Bowes-Lyon, born in a stately home on August 4th, 1900, could be more accurately described as "the reluctant Queen," since she never sought the role that was ultimately hers. Indeed, she has admitted that the thought of becoming a member of the Royal Family frightened her. Yet even when she married "dear Bertie" in 1923, the possibility of his becoming King George VI seemed remote. Twice, because of her fears and self-doubts, she refused the man whose love for her was to last more than 32 years.

Born a few months before the Victorian era ended, she has lived through an age of change. At the time of her birth, air travel was a dream, Socialism and Communism were embryonic, Marconi was years away from making the real breakthrough with wireless, the map of Europe included countries and kingdoms that no longer exist, and there were still vast tracts of the world not yet trod upon. Nylon and antibiotics were not even a dream. It was an era of carriage-and-pairs, gaslit streets. In 1905, as a five-year-old, she met the boy who was to become her husband 18 years later. From her family's London home at 20, St James's Square, she went to a party at Montague House — one of the last private homes in Whitehall. There she met Prince Albert, the boy who became King George VI. They were to meet many times at her Scottish home, and in the London house.

And Queen she was to be. The die was cast when she finally said "Yes" to Prince Albert at her home, St Paul's, Walden Bury, Hertfordshire, on January 14th, 1923, having turned down his earlier proposals of marriage in 1921 and 1922. At the time she probably looked back with a quiet chuckle to a day at Glamis Castle in August 1910 when a gipsy told her: "One day you'll be a Queen." Ten-year-old Lady Elizabeth Bowes-Lyon looked forward to the three months the family spent in their Scottish home. And this year there was to be a garden party. She visited all the sideshows — and the gipsy's tent. With a giggle she told her French governess: "The gipsy was silly. Who wants to be a Queen?"

The governess, Mlle Lang, told her young charge: "That would not be possible unless they changed the laws for you." No one would have guessed that 26 years later the gipsy would be proved correct. She hit the right note with the public from the start of her marriage to Albert, the then Duke of York. It was 1923, and the devastating losses of World War One were still fresh in the minds of the people, so, when the bride paused as she walked down the aisle at Westminster Abbey and laid her bouquet of white York roses and Scottish heather on the Tomb of the Unknown Warrior, everyone was moved.

It is unlikely that on her wedding day Elizabeth fully realised what she was letting herself in for. The truth probably began to dawn when she returned from her honeymoon to the largest pile of mail she had ever received. It suddenly seemed that everyone needed her. There were requests for her patronage from charities and societies, invitations to open everything from local fetes to hospital wards, and appeals for visits and personal appearances. Elizabeth took to public engagements as if she had been training for them all her life. Relaxed, happy and natural in front of a crowd, it became clear that she had a special gift for endearing herself to the people. She soon became known as "the Smiling Duchess." She was a great success publicly, but behind the scenes she was working on another of her Royal duties. The Duke of York had suffered since childhood from a nervous stammer that made his obligatory public speeches a terrible ordeal.

With a world tour approaching in January 1927, during which the Duke would have to make numerous speeches, Elizabeth decided they must do something positive about his problem. They found a speech therapist and Elizabeth persuaded her husband to see him. The first appointment proved so encouraging that for two and a half months towards the end of 1926 he visited the man almost every day. Elizabeth would watch as her husband went through the exercises and help him repeat them at home. Within a month there was a dramatic improvement, and the Duke could look forward to the world tour with confidence.

However, Elizabeth had mixed feeling about the tour. Her first child, Princess Elizabeth, was only nine months old, yet the Duchess was being asked to sacrifice six precious months away from her baby. The parting from the nursery was so distressing that the car had to be driven twice around the block while Elizabeth composed herself.

When they returned home and King George V's health failed and his eldest son, David, the Prince of Wales — later the exiled Duke of Windsor — grew ever-more irresponsible, the Yorks were called upon more frequently to represent the Royal Family on official engagements. The old King wished that his second son, and not his first, should succeed him. His only comfort was that, since the Prince of Wales showed no sign of marrying and having children, the Duke of York's daughter, Elizabeth, would one day inherit the Throne.

Eventually, of course his dearest wish did come true. Within a year of his death on January 20th, 1936, his eldest son abdicated to marry Wallis Simpson, and the Duke of York succeeded as King George VI. It was a sudden and daunting responsibility. "This is absolutely terrible," the new King wailed to his cousin, Lord Mountbatten. "I never wanted this to happen. I'm quite unprepared for it. David has been trained for all this all his life. I've never even seen a State Paper. I'm only a Naval Officer."

Elizabeth stepped in once more, calming his nerves, soothing his fears and assuring him of her help. Like her husband, she had never wanted such a role but, since it had been thrust upon them, she knew where her duty lay. The task was to prove more demanding than the Royal Couple ever expected. All over Europe monarchies had crashed and the Abdication crisis threw the whole future of our own Monarchy into doubt. George VI and his Queen had not only to establish a new reign, but also to re-establish the popularity of the very Crown itself.

To add to their problems, war broke out. Yet although horrifying, the war was to bring them closer to the people than ever before. Blitzed and fearful, Britons were especially impressed when Queen Elizabeth dismissed advice from Ministers and Palace aides that the Royal children should be sent to safety in Canada. Elizabeth declared: "The Princesses would never leave without me and I couldn't leave without the King, and the King will never leave."

The couple were soon plunged into a heavier workload than ever before. They toured the country, visiting bombed cities, inspecting munitions factories, and they went around devastated ruins in the East End of London. Churchill told Elizabeth in 1940: "This war has drawn the Throne and people more closely together than ever before. Your Majesties are more beloved by all classes than any of the princes of the past." By the end of the war, the King and Queen had won the love of their people, but sadly they did not have long to enjoy peace and security together. Just seven years later, in 1952, George VI, worn out by illness and overwork, died at Sandringham.

For more than 60 years she has endeared herself to succeeding generations, first as Duchess of York, when she demonstrated her keen interest in the world around her; then as the Queen who brought the Throne closer to the people; and finally as the Monarch's widow who relished being called the Queen Mum.

THANK HEAVEN FOR LITTLE GIRLS!

ELIZABETH, the Queen Mother, is a living history of the Twentieth Century — a unique witness of events that make our times. This year marks the fiftieth year since she became a Queen. When she was born, Queen Victoria was still alive and Britain's last great colonial war was being fought against the Boers in South Africa. She now flies about the world in jets and helicopters — she once clocked 30,000 miles in a year. Yet the Wright Brothers were still experimenting in their bicycle shed at the time of her birth. They did not make their first powered flight until three years later.

Six years were to pass before Emily Pankhurst began her suffragette movement, and another 28 years before women got the vote. She has seen wars, disasters, revolutions, lands discovered, conquered and lost, dictators, kings and presidents come and go, the map of the world re-written and re-written again, industrial depressions, great days of glory . . . and her world change from a well ordered, class-conscious society to the anything-goes days of the late Twentieth Century.

But the rules that governed her day were formed in the Victorian era, when no one called on anyone else without first sending around a card; when the upper-class father paid £1,000 for the hire of a London house for "the season" — the equivalent of £20,000 today; when another £50 — around £1,000 in the 1980s — would go on each of his womenfolk's clothes.

Those were the days when the debutantes and even their less financially favoured sisters, were strictly chaperoned to ensure that they went up the aisles whiter and purer than a Barbara Cartland heroine in that pre extra-marital sex, pre-Pill era. A "swinger," and of course there was no such word in those days, was said to be "headstrong" and watched by mamas, aunts and other chaperones to prevent any hanky-panky amidst the aspidistra plants.

It is a reflection of the times that most of the young men who died in the First World War had never known about "It" before they went to the trenches — and usually their deaths. When the Queen Mother was a young girl there were very properly managed debutante and hunt balls at which a young man literally begged to be put on a girl's dance card: none of the casual disco eroticism. The social calendar dictated that the London summer season of balls and fashionable dinners was to be followed by migration to Scotland or Yorkshire for grouse shooting in August. The hunting shires were the venues of November and winter, and early spring would be spent in the South of France until the new season began in April.

Whether getting the sun at Cannes or Southend, there was really only one future for a woman — to marry. It was considered that she owed this to herself and the family that had brought her up and trained her for a career in the kitchen, bedroom and nursery. That was the society into which Elizabeth was born. How times have changed!

Her formal title is Queen Elizabeth the Queen Mother — but she is affectionately known throughout the world as plain "Queen Mum", a global granny smiling her way into the hearts of heaven knows how many children who feel that they too could clamber up on her knee for a bedtime story. That warmth, over so many years, has spread across continents and today been returned over and over.

No one, of course, ever knows the innermost thoughts of a woman who never wanted to be Queen. When she was being wooed by the man who was to become King George the Sixth, she confided in her family and friends that she was wary of marrying a King's son: she feared the enormous responsibilities that such a partnership would bring . . . fears that were to be justified. The fact that she sat alongside her Sovereign came about because of an odd quirk of history — the abdication of the Duke of Windsor as Edward VIII, the uncrowned Monarch. Had she believed in fortune tellers, she would have known her fate from the age of seven, when a gipsy held her hand and told her that one day she would be Queen.

Despite neither wanting, nor expecting, the role, she proved through the years of crises, turmoil and pain that marked the late King's Reign that she was one of the finest Royal Consorts Britain could ever have hoped for.

Lady Elizabeth Bowes-Lyon became the first wholly British Queen for centuries, and the first Scottish Queen the English have ever had.

For centuries her family had provided spouses for the sons of kings and aristocrats. Her background was one where anxious mamas made sure that their daughters were of suitable charm, grace and iron-willed fibre to be chased by only the best suitors. Then, as now, though with less acreage in the gossip columns, the parents of such "gels" pushed their laced, delicate and demure, witty — but not too witty — daughters to the front of Society, hoping for the best "catch."

Elizabeth Angela Marguerite Bowes-Lyon, the Lady Elizabeth Glamis, was the third daughter of the Earl and Countess of Strathmore and Kinghome. Her father had a Scottish ancestry dating back to Robert the Bruce; her mother, Nina Cecilia, was of English stock. She was the daughter of the Reverend Charles William Cavendish-Bentinck, a cousin of the Duke of Portland. Among her ancestors was one wretched Lady Glamis who was burned alive as a "witch" in Edinburgh in 1540.

The Bowes-Lyon name comes from the Eighteenth Century, when a rich County Durham industrialist, George Bowes, agreed to get the Strathmore family out of debt. The Ninth Earl wished to marry Bowes' daughter, Eleanor. The dowry that went with her was Bowes' entire fortune and all his estates in the North and in Hertfordshire. In exchange for the wealth and hand in marriage of such a valuable daughter the Strathmore family name of Lyon had to be changed to Bowes. After the old boy died the name quickly became Bowes-Lyon.

The Queen Mother's father was a quiet, kindly, religious man. As Lord Lieutenant of Forfar he lived the classic role of an Anglo-Scottish gentleman of his day, concerned mainly with shooting, cricket and forestry. His wife had the greatest influence on their youngest daughter. The Countess of Strathmore was a strait-laced lady interested in embroidery and music. She was so accomplished musically that she could attend a concert, return home, go to the piano and play the pieces from memory. She is said to have been a lively woman with a great sense of humour . . . qualities that her daughter has inherited in abundance.

When she was in her twenties, Lady Elizabeth was to write a story about the everyday life of a little girl . . . it was a tale that bore a strong resemblance to her own childhood: "At the bottom of the garden is the wood — the haunt of fairies, with its anemones and ponds, and moss-grown statues . . . whenever — and this is often — a dead bird is found in this enchanted wood it is often given solemn burial in a small box lined with rose-leaves."

"Now it is time to go haymaking, which means getting very hot in a delicious smell. Very often she gets up wonderfully early — about six o'clock — to feed her chickens and make sure they are safe. The hens stubbornly insist on laying their eggs in a place called the flea house, where she and her brother go and hide from Nurse . . ."

Much of Lady Elizabeth's childhood was spent at Glamis, the old Scottish castle dating back to the Fourteenth Century. It was here that the teenager discovered interests which lasted throughout her life: playing cricket and tennis; developing into an accomplished gardener, and becoming skilful at fly fishing. She also saw the horrors of war at Glamis in

1914-18, when the castle was turned into a convalescent home for wounded soldiers.

She was too young to be a nurse, but helped as best she could by serving meals to the wounded, writing their letters, playing cards with them or just cheering them up as a fun-loving, pretty girl; an art she did not seem to ever lose. These bitter days gave her an understanding of the world of ordinary folk; of people she would normally have never met as a daughter of the Upper Class.

She became aware of how the war brought, for a brief period, a sense of common feeling to a class-ridden nation: four of her brothers were wounded — one of them was killed. The memories of that time remained with her always — hence what many today still recall as the "common touch" — though the world she belonged to returned to its exclusiveness, its pleasures and its aristocratic goings-on soon after the Armistice.

The Strathmores, with a fortune worth nearly a million pounds — the equivalent today of £20,000,000 — resumed their conventional parental role of launching their daughter on Society. And what a launch! She startled London and Scottish society when she came on the scene. Contemporary pictures show her as an imp-eyed, petite (5 ft. 2 in.) beauty, trim of waist, with gentle mouth and soft jawline. Her blue eyes were described as brilliant, her skin and complexion lovely. Her peaches-and-cream look — inherited by her daughters — has been the envy of most women throughout her life. By the time she made her debut at Court she was already turning heads as a striking, dark-haired 19-year-old. Drawing-room gossip of the time praised her as being irresistible to men.

There was more . . . much more. She had the reputation of being full of high spirits, one of the best ballroom dancers of the early 1920s, and her company much sought after. She was once praised as "a sweet-faced, pretty and gentle-natured girl". No one could argue with that. Her entry into the heart of Royal circles came about through her being on Girl Guides committees. Princess Mary (later Lady Harewood) the only daughter of King George V and Queen Mary, was a keen Guide and befriended the Scottish lass. She invited her to Buckingham Palace, where she

soon attracted the attentions of the eldest of the two Royal sons, 26-year-old David, and 25-year-old Albert.

The King and Queen were looking around anxiously for suitable brides for their sons, particularly David. The Lady Elizabeth Bowes-Lyon, the delightful friend of daughter Mary, fitted the bill perfectly. A year after Lady Elizabeth was introduced to the Royal Family, Queen Mary, who was staying near Glamis, drove over to her Scottish home. Rumours began to fly that a suitable girl had been found to steady the gadabout Prince of Wales.

But it was not David who became deeply interested in her — it was Albert, a less dashing creature than his brother. His health was not good. He suffered from a stammer which occasionally caused bouts of anger and made him shy socially. Yet he was good-looking, a fine tennis player, rode well and could be kind and considerate. Overshadowed by his popular elder brother, Bertie became involved, through his friendship with the Bowes-Lyon brothers, with the delightful Lady Elizabeth. Her kindness and patience helped him overcome his initial nervousness and uncertainty. So much so that a few months after Bertie spent a weekend at Glamis Castle Queen Mary confided to a friend that her son "is very much attracted to Lady Elizabeth Bowes-Lyon. He's always talking about her."

The gamin-like young Bowes-Lyon soon took a liking to the Duke of York. After spending one of several weekends at Glamis Castle with her, the Duke told his mother: "The more I see Elizabeth the more I like her." In fact he had fallen madly in love with her, but it was some time before Elizabeth agreed to marry him. She had that wariness of marrying a king's son.

Although she was happy and at ease in "Bertie's" company, the thought of exchanging a quiet country life for the public glare of an unceasing round of Royal duties was something that needed thinking about.

When Bertie began pursuing her his family thought he was doomed to disappointment: "You'll be a lucky fellow if she accepts you," warned King George. Elizabeth had no shortage of suitors. When the Prince first proposed to her, she refused him. Bertie continued to pay court in London and in Scotland, and slowly he dissolved her doubts, so that after three proposals and two years of persistent courtship, he was able to telegraph his parents, "*All right. Bertie.*" "Bertie is supremely happy," Queen Mary wrote after the bride-to-be had stayed at Sandringham.

True, she was a commoner, but, as their elder son, David, the natural successor to the Throne, was thought certain to marry a suitable person and produce an heir of his own, they thought this would not be a problem.

In fact elder brother David gave her a hint of what was to happen during the Abdication thirteen years later, when she expressed her doubts about marrying Albert George. The future Duke of Windsor told Elizabeth: "You had better take him and go on in the end to Buck House."

It was much later, after George VI's death, that her true feelings about the marriage became clear. She agreed to marry him, but only out of a sense of duty. "I fell in love with him afterwards," she revealed to a friend a few years ago. Lady Strathmore, Elizabeth's mother, noticed the struggle she was having with her conscience, and noted: "That winter was their first time I have known Elizabeth really worried. I think she was torn between her longing to make Bertie happy and her reluctance to take on the big responsibilities which this marriage must bring."

Bertie seemed confused as well. Lady Strathmore felt sorry for him: "I do hope he will find a nice wife who will make him happy. I like him so much and he is a man who will be made or marred by his wife."

According to the Duke of Windsor her influence was that of "a refreshing spirit." She even managed to persuade George V and Queen Mary to play charades, to laugh and to relax a little.

A date was fixed for the wedding at Westminster Abbey — April 26th, 1923, the first time in almost 500 years that a Prince of the Royal House had been married there. The last was King Richard II in 1382. Then followed a dispute among the Royal advisers and Church leaders about the rank and status of the future Duchess of York, for it was rare for a son of the King of England to marry a commoner, albeit such a well-connected one. Some voices were raised against allowing the marriage at all, but these were silenced for a number of sound reasons. One was that the British had just come through a bitter war with a Germany led by a cousin of the Royal Family, Kaiser Bill. There was considerable opposition, therefore, towards further links with foreign royalty. So a home-grown bride was a popular choice.

Elizabeth's friend, Princess Mary, married the Earl of Harewood — still classed as a commoner despite his grand title and estates in Yorkshire. This helped to break the ground for another person of less-than-regal blue blood to be welcomed into the fold. But above all, it was argued that the Heir to the Throne, David, Prince of Wales, would surely soon mend his dashing ways and settle down and raise a family. The offspring of the new Duke and Duchess of York would not be in line for the Throne anyway . . . would they?

Their wedding was an occasion for one of the first signs of national cheer in a country just beginning to live again after the horrors of the First World War. The streets were packed with happy crowds for the bride as she drove by in a dress of a simple medieval style with a square neckline made of fine chiffon. On loan from Queen Mary was a train of old Flanders lace, which had beneath it a longer train of Nottingham lace. There was massive unemployment, with thousands out of work in the lace trade, and this gesture was made in the hope it might boost their business.

ANOTHER INDICATION of the Establishment's awareness of the harsh world of the working classes was the guest list. Among the three thousand seated in Westminster Abbey were thirty apprentices from factories throughout Britain who had been invited and provided with new suits by the Duke of York, president of the well-meaning Industrial Welfare Society . . . an earlier version of the Duke of Edinburgh's Award Scheme.

Perhaps the Archbishop of York, the Most Rev. Cosmo Lang, foresaw the hard years ahead in his wedding address: "You, dear bride, in your Scottish home, have grown up from childhood among country folk and friendship with them has been your native air. So have you both been fitted for your place in the people's life and your separate lives are now, till death, made one. You cannot resolve that your wedded life will be happy, but you can and will resolve that it shall be noble . . . the warm and generous heart of this people takes you today into itself. Will you not, in response, take that heart, with all its joys and sorrows, into your own?"

The young Elizabeth instinctively hit the right note with the public from the start. The devastating losses of the First World War were still fresh in the minds of the people, so, when the bride paused as she walked down the aisle and laid her bouquet of white York roses and Scottish heather on the Tomb of the Unknown Warrior, everyone was moved. But the honeymoon was hardly a romantic affair. Much of it was spent at Glamis, in biting wind, rain and snow and Elizabeth ended up confined to bed with whooping cough.

Her new father-in-law quickly showed his affection towards the young bride. King George wrote to his son a few weeks after the marriage: "The better I know and the more I see of your dear little wife, the more charming I think she is, and everyone feels in love with her here." But the new Duchess's own family were not, as one might expect, over excited with pride that she had hooked one of the best catches of her generation. A relative summed up their attitude when he merely said: "Thank God she has married a good man."

From the moment of his marriage, Bertie became the King's favourite son. George had mellowed from his earlier harsh attitude towards his family: "My father was frightened of his mother, I was frightened of my father, and I am damned well going to see to it that my children are frightened of me," he used to declare. His sons were said to be petrified of him.

Bertie, the first of four brothers to be married, received fatherly approval. Even Queen Mary, as cold a parent as her husband, began to soften. She became devoted to her first daughter-in-law, whom she described as "the pretty Strathmore girl." But at first it wasn't all plain sailing, and settling down was not the easiest of tasks for the new bride. In spite of Queen Mary's approbation, Elizabeth was bothered in the first few months of married life by what can only be described as mother-in-law trouble.

The wives of her sons, as Mary saw it so long ago, had to learn to bow to her wishes. But, as she saw how happy Bertie became with his bride, the formidable old Queen mellowed and, over the years, developed a close, kindly, almost loving relationship with Elizabeth. With the King it had been that way from the beginning. Her relations with him were very happy. By nature a gruff man, given occasionally to harsh words, George V was charmed into submission by the young bride. She was to write after his death: "Unlike his own children I was never afraid of him. In all his twelve years of having me as a daughter-in-law he never spoke one unkind or abrupt word to me and was always ready to listen and give advice on one's own silly little affairs. When he was in the mood he could be deliciously funny, too."

Although she was warmly accepted into the Royal Family Elizabeth still had to endure the strict formality of George and Mary's Court, in sharp contrast to the very easy-going life among her own folk. She had to get used to a strict and "proper" regime. Going to the palaces of her in-laws, for instance, even for a close family gathering, was always a matter of great formality, when everyone dressed correctly for whatever time of day it might be. A small lunch or supper was, inevitably, a very stiff affair.

Slowly, Elizabeth started changing much of this. She began softly and gently by persuading the King and Queen to let her play the piano at after-dinner gatherings, starting with a few classic pieces, then moving on to sing popular ballads — and getting the others to join in!

She also changed her husband. Her gaiety and abundance of self-confidence began to rub off on him. The socially shy and highly strung young man, ashamed of his stammer, was transformed in a few years to an outward-going self-confident public figure, backed by a wife who encouraged him to have faith in himself.

Elizabeth, too, swiftly became a public figure in her own right and the world came to know, for the first time, the warmth of that famous smile. As she went about visiting hospitals, attending meetings to raise money for the poor or taking part in ceremonial duties she always appeared to be thoroughly enjoying herself. *The Times* once commented: "She lays a foundation stone as if she has just discovered a new and delightful way of spending an afternoon."

She liked meeting people, and seemed always interested in their business, no matter how humble. Many of those who today talk about "that lovely lady" are thinking about the young Elizabeth and her wanderings about the country in the years of the Depression. She had a gift of seeming to smile at every individual in a group or crowd and the smile seemed to be a personal recognition.

The new Duchess of York — as Elizabeth became after the wedding — and Bertie, who took up the title of Duke of York as an alternative to Prince Albert, made, as their first "official" home, White Lodge, a rambling old house in Richmond Park, eight miles South-West of Buckingham Palace, although they liked to be near their friends in the "smart-set" quarter of London, in this age of the "flapper" 1920s. As society leaders Elizabeth and Bertie flung themselves into the wildness of nightclub life.

They spent most of their newly-wed days at the London home of Elizabeth's parents, No. 17 Bruton Street, W1, a fashionable thoroughfare linking Berkeley Square with Bond Street. So it was here, three years after their wedding, that the Yorks had their first child. The fact that she was a girl disappointed King George, who had hoped his first grandchild would be a boy.

Apart from having two surgeons in attendance at the birth, the 26-year-old Duchess also had at hand the Home Secretary of the day, Sir William Joynson Hicks. That one of the Government's senior Ministers was present was because of a tradition going back almost 300 years. An antiquated requirement, completely out of place in the Twentieth Century but insisted upon, following the wrangling at the time of Mary of Modena, Consort of the maligned Roman Catholic James II. She was believed to be incapable of child-bearing but had born a son in July, 1688. Shocked at the thought of another Papist on the Throne, the Protestant Whigs had falsely denounced the child as a foundling smuggled into the Queen's bed-chamber in a warming-pan.

Since that time it had become customary for someone responsible to Parliament to guarantee the legitimate claims of a possible Heir to the Throne. This was to be the last time such an indelicate Parliamentary intrusion was to take place. For instance, Queen Elizabeth II did not have to submit herself to this scrutiny when Prince Charles and her other children were born in a more enlightened era.

With Parliamentary approval, the baby who would one day be Queen arrived, and an official announcement was made: "Her Royal Highness the Duchess of York was safely delivered of a Princess (at 2.40 a.m.) this morning. Both mother and daughter are doing well." King George and Queen Mary had left instructions that they were to be told right away if there were any developments at Bruton Street. So it was that in the small hours of Wednesday, April 21st, duty equerry Captain Reginald Seymour obeyed orders and roused the King and Queen to tell them the news. "We were awakened at 4.00 a.m.," wrote Queen Mary, at Windsor, "and Reggie Seymour informed us that darling Elizabeth had got a daughter at 2.40. Such a relief and joy."

That afternoon Mary and George arrived at Bruton Street to be told that the young mother was asleep. "We saw the baby," Queen Mary wrote again, delighted with her first grand-daughter. "A little darling with a lovely complexion and fair hair." Other first visitors described the Duchess's first baby as "possessing fair hair, large dark-lashed blue eyes" and "tiny ears set close to a well shaped head." The Queen also thought the child was enchanting, but she wished the baby was "more like your little mother."

In a letter to his mother a few days later Bertie gushed like any proud father: "You don't know what a tremendous joy it is to Elizabeth and me to have our little girl," he wrote. "We always wanted a child to make our happiness complete, and now that it has happened, it seems so wonderful and strange.

I am so proud of Elizabeth at this moment after all she has gone through during the last few days, and I am so thankful that everything has happened as it should and so successfully. I do hope you and Papa are as delighted as we are to have a grand-daughter, or would you have sooner had a grandson? May I say I hope you won't spoil her when she gets a bit older."

The next day, though, newspapers were not as ecstatic as the Princely father. They gave the Royal Birth second place to developments in the General Strike. The child arrived in the middle of industrial strife. Troops were encamped not far from her cot in Hyde Park to cope with the emergency. On May 3rd the country was thrown into chaos by the nation-wide strike, and Britain was virtually paralysed for ten days.

Another reason why the newspapers were not dutifully delighted was that there was no reason why the birth of a daughter to the Duke and Duchess of York should have any special significance. She was not in the direct line of succession. Once Uncle David, the Prince of Wales, had married and begun a family, and indeed once the Yorks had a few boys themselves, this child would be a complete outside runner as a possible Heir to the Throne. For of course Prince Albert ranked below his elder brother in Royal precedence. Therefore, back in 1926, it seemed far-fetched to link this new baby Princess with the Throne. Her only chance of becoming a Queen in the future was probably as the wife of some foreign king. But for the time being she was third in the order of succession.

As the Duchess recovered from the strains of a difficult confinement, she and Bertie settled down to discuss what names they should choose for their daughter. They wanted "Elizabeth" as a link with the mother, but they were worried that the King — a final arbiter on these matters — would not approve. Prince Albert wrote to his father: "Such a nice name. I am sure there will be no muddle over two Elizabeths in the family and there has been no one of that name in your family for a long time. Elizabeth of York sounds so nice, too." King George replied with his approval for all the names chosen. "Alexandra" remembered his own mother and "Mary" complimented his sister, Princess Mary. As for "Elizabeth," he said he thought this was "such a pretty name."

"I have heard from Bertie," he told Queen Mary. "He mentions Elizabeth Alexandra Mary. I quite approve and will tell him so."

The christening took place in the private chapel of Buckingham Palace on May 29th. It was performed by the Archbishop of York and was an essentially quiet family affair, attended by parents, grandparents and godparents. Traditional "Royal Water" from the River Jordan was used from the gold lily font made for the christening of Vicky, Princess Royal, in 1840. "Of course poor baby cried," Queen Mary wrote afterwards. The crying baby was dressed in the cream satin robe overlaid with Honiton lace that had been worn by nearly all of Queen Victoria's children.

The Duchess of York breast-fed her baby for the first month, then, having to resume official duties, handed her into the arms of Mrs. Clara Knight, who had been her own nanny. With the help of a nursery-maid Mrs. Knight fed, dressed and exercised the new baby Princess and, twice a day, presented her in a clean dress to her adoring parents. When the little girl woke up crying in the night it was the nursery staff who went to comfort her. Mrs. Knight's Christian name was Clara, but this defeated most of her charges, who could only manage "Alla" — and this remained the name by which Princess Elizabeth knew her.

Mrs Knight was an old-fashioned nanny, a family retainer in the traditional style, whose whole life was her work, welcoming the role of surrogate mother put on her by her employers, delighting in the challenge of coping with everything, and scarcely ever taking a holiday or even a day off.

FOR MOST COUPLES there should have followed an idyllic period of settling down together as a family with their first child. Not for the Yorks. The baby was barely eight months old when the Duke and

Duchess were sent to Australia and New Zealand on an official tour. It was to be their first major public duty together in the Empire — and for that they had to abandon their first child in London for six months in the hands of Nanny Knight. The Duchess trusted Mrs. Knight, but like any first-time mother she worried over leaving her child behind.

Which was why in the weeks before departure she spent as much time as possible with Princess Elizabeth. When the Duchess and Bertie were leaving to board the battleship *Renown* for their journey across the globe the young mum went back twice to kiss her baby after she had placed Elizabeth in the nurse's arms in the hallway. On the way to the railway station from Bruton Street the chauffeur had to circle Grosvenor Gardens twice so that Elizabeth could recover her composure before facing the crowds.

Throughout the tour cables were sent each week to the anxious parents giving news of their daughter. A photographer took pictures of the child so that they would miss as little as possible of their daughter's progress. These little touches helped, but how many mothers could endure the first few months of their child's life in this way? "We are not supposed to be human," observed the Duchess sadly.

Nevertheless the tour was a huge success, much of it due to Elizabeth. Bertie had to make several speeches, and, with that stammer of his, every one was an ordeal. The Duke of York had suffered since childhood from a nervous stammer that made his obligatory public speeches something to dread. But as the world tour approached, Elizabeth decided to do something positive about his problem. She persuaded her husband to see a speech therapist in Harley Street, an Australian called Lionel Logue. The first appointment proved so encouraging that for two-and-a-half months towards the end of 1926, he visited Logue almost every day. Elizabeth would watch as her husband went through the exercises and help him repeat them carefully at home.

Within a month there was a dramatic improvement, and the Duke was able to look forward to the world tour with confidence. Each evening Elizabeth would help him to rehearse a speech for the next day . . . then,

when he was making the delivery, sit on the platform or stage looking straight ahead pretending not to notice if he struggled to get out his words.

This strong, silent support in public and her painstaking help in private eventually brought the reward of almost-perfect diction in the end — but it took many years to achieve. The public never suspected the personal strain behind the Duchess's smile as the tour went happily along. The Duke found new authority and confidence with his speech, and Elizabeth, as ever, charmed everyone.

When they returned from their first overseas tour — and everywhere they went she was a sensation — Elizabeth was reunited with a daughter who had grown to twice the size. The Royal pair, united as a proper family at last, then spent three blissful years together in their new home at 145 Piccadilly.

These were the days of the flappers . . . the Roaring Twenties . . . the Charleston and daring new American cocktails. Their new home was bang in the middle of a startling new wave of nightlife and they joined in briefly with the rest of the "darlings" of their generation, dining out in public and going to neighbourhood nightclubs, though Elizabeth, with her love of dancing, had more enthusiasm for this way of life than Bertie.

Number 145, four doors away from Apsley House, the "Iron" Duke of Wellington's mansion, had been prepared for the couple while they were away. Until the Duke acquired the lease it had stood empty for several years. Alas, the tall, four-storeyed building, faced with grey stone and built in 1875, no longer exists.

Life at 145 was described as follows by a Royal courtier: "When Princess Elizabeth's nurse, descending to the morning room or the drawing room, says in her quiet tones, 'I think it is bed time now, Elizabeth,' there are no poutings or protests, just a few last minute laughs at mummy's delicious bed time jokes, and then Princess Elizabeth's hand slips into her nurse's hand, and the two go off gaily together across the deep chestnut pile of the hall carpet to the accommodating lift, which in two seconds has whisked them up to the familiar dear domain which is theirs to hold and to share."

The house had no private garden but shared with its neighbours a communal area of lawn and bushes known as Hamilton Gardens. Here the young mother played games with the Princess, sometimes being joined by father. In the upstairs nursery were the "stables" for the collection of rocking-horses, which required "exercise", "grooming" and "feeding." Every evening young Elizabeth would change their saddles and harness before going to bed.

It was during these happy "toddler days" that the childhood name that has stuck with our present Queen Elizabeth among her own family came about. She could not pronounce "Elizabeth" properly so she became "Lilibet." She was "re-christened" Lilibet by King George V who was so charmed by her stumbling attempts to handle the pronunciation of her first name.

Four years later the Yorks' second child came along. In view of what happened in a stormy later life that is now so well publicised, it might seem almost appropriate that Princess Margaret Rose was born on a day of thunder and lightning.

The Duchess gave birth to Margaret at Glamis Castle on August 21st, 1930 — the first member of the Royal Family to be born in Scotland for more than 300 years. While the weary mother sought only to recuperate in peace, the local pipe band celebrated the event noisily by marching about the neighbourhood with a small army of villagers, who rounded off the day with a bonfire on a nearby hill. Fortunately the Queen Mother likes the sound of the pipes.

They were so confident that the child would be a boy that Elizabeth and Bertie had given little thought to girls' names, but within a week they had decided that their daughter should be called Ann Margaret. But the King did not like the name Ann and would not even approve changing to Margaret Ann. The Duchess pleaded with Queen Mary for her help. She wrote to her: "I am very anxious to call her Ann Margaret as I think that Ann of York sounds pretty, and Elizabeth and Ann go so well together. I wonder what you think? Lots of people have suggested Margaret, but it has no family links really on either side."

But George would not be moved, so eventually another letter, this time of capitulation, was sent. "Bertie and I have decided now to call our little daughter "Margaret Rose" instead of M. Ann, as Papa does not like Ann. I hope you like it. I think that it is very pretty together."

The sister's response to the new arrival was: "I've got a baby sister, Margaret Rose, and I'm going to call her Bud. She's not a real rose yet, is she? She's only a bud." There were some suggestions in Royal and political circles that Margaret and Elizabeth should now hold equal rank in the Line of Accession. George would not have this. Shortly after the christening, the King announced the order as he saw it. Heir to the Throne, David, Prince of Wales, followed (subject to change if he should have children) by the Duke of York. Next in line was Princess Elizabeth, while Margaret Rose occupied fourth place ahead of the King's two younger sons, the Duke of Gloucester and Prince George, later Duke of Kent. If Bertie and Elizabeth of York should have a son, that would alter the pecking order once more.

After the arrival of Margaret, it was suggested that the Duke of York go to Ottawa as the next Governor-General. It would have been a highly popular move if the Yorks had lived in Canada with their two little girls. The King's advisers, Sir Clive Wigram and Lord Stamfordham, both approved the prospect, but it was disallowed by Mr. J. H. Thomas, the Dominions Secretary of State in the Labour Cabinet, much to the Duchess's relief.

The two sisters were also a great joy to their grandfather. While the Yorks were living in Piccadilly, the Duchess would occasionally hold the eldest child at an upstairs window so that she could wave good-morning to her grandfather standing at a window half a mile away across Green Park in Buckingham Palace.

The West End address was useful for being near the rest of the family and their society friends, but the excitement of the nightclub life began to wear off: Elizabeth and Bertie wanted a more well-ordered and tranquil life in surroundings suitable for bringing up children.

In truth, life for the two girls was becoming too public. If they wanted to go for a walk or just play among flowers, trees and ducks, they had to do so under the gaze of the staring crowds in Hyde Park or Battersea Park. They became such public property that passengers would go on the top deck of buses to look down into the back garden of 145.

It was then that their parents came to the conclusion that they must find somewhere more private outside London. Number 145 though was still the house that the Duchess regarded as her own first home. She added all the right touches, double-glazed windows — an innovation at that time — hushed the passing traffic, and it was a house of pleasant sound. A Georgian clock chimed a carillon of sixteen bells and Australian canaries sang near a garden door. It remained the Yorks' London home for nearly ten years. But the pressure was on them for the sake of the children to find a quiet retreat.

That was how Royal Lodge in Windsor Great Park, given to them by the King and Queen, became a country retreat. It was once occupied by the Prince Regent in the early Nineteenth Century and was in a bad state of repair. Even the gardens needed seeing to, but the Yorks grabbed the chance of taking over the Lodge, for, like any other young couple, they wanted to create their own home from home.

T HE DUCHESS was enraptured by the possibilities of the dilapidated old house and wilderness of a garden. The Duke was less enthusiastic. A lot of work needed to be done, but he was none the less grateful to his father for giving it to them, and pleased for his wife. She knew that the children would be excited at the prospect of a house with such a big garden to play in.

"It is too kind of you to have offered us Royal Lodge," the Duke wrote to his father, who replied that he was pleased they liked it but he hoped they would call it *The* Royal Lodge, by which name it had been known ever since George IV built it in the early 1800s. There can be any number of Royal Lodges, but only one known as "The Royal Lodge." The Duke stuck to his father's

wishes, but over the years the prefix has been dropped and plain Royal Lodge it is.

The Duchess adored the privacy and solitude of the grounds and saw the possibilities of restoring and improving the house itself. "Having seen it I think it will suit us admirably," she said.

The building and grounds not only became a weekend retreat but their favourite house as Elizabeth jumped into the task of being a country-wife and home-maker, choosing furniture, picking curtains, stocking her kitchens, ordering a coat of fresh paint here, new wallpaper there. It might have been a bit too chintzy for modern tastes, but she turned a neglected, scruffy old dwelling into a snug hideaway of domestic bliss. Making the place habitable took them more than a year.

Royal Lodge became the Yorks' favourite residence. The centrepiece of the house was a great banqueting salon dating from Regency times. Beneath a ceiling twenty feet high this room measured forty-eight feet in length and almost thirty feet in width. By comparison the rest of the house was modest in proportions. Two wings were added later by the Duke and Duchess, one to provide bedrooms, bathrooms and sitting rooms for themselves and the other to form the nursery and accommodation for guests. Servants' quarters were built above the garage and in the grounds an open-air swimming pool. Here the York children grew up in a happy family environment.

The entire family had to "muck-in" and sort out the garden, which was a disordered mess of weeds and thorn bushes. Elizabeth and Margaret were given their own special part to work on, though neither of them developed the same enthusiasm for horticulture that their mother shows even today. When the Duke expanded the garden of Royal Lodge from fifteen to ninety acres, they all joined in the task of clearing the wilderness.

The King and Queen arrived one weekend to be conducted behind a wheelbarrow, pushed by a dirt-stained Princess Elizabeth, to a newly planted tree, beneath which was to be found her father wielding a pair of secateurs.

Windsor was where the Royal Family's "doggie" lineage began. Those famous corgies began to enter the scene. The first of the long line was introduced — Rozavel Golden Eagle, known to the family as "Cookie." The Duchess had grown up with dogs around her and she thought her children should have their company, too.

Here there was laughter and fun away from servants, where mother could cook simple meals in her own kitchen. At bath-time the giggling youngsters would fling soapsuds around, sometimes catching the eyes of mum and dad. And, of course, always at the end of it all, the Duchess would read the girls bed-time nursery stories, and later, when they were old enough, teach them to read. Royal Lodge was a place of laughter and happiness which spilled into every nook and cranny of that rambling building. No wonder, when the Queen Mother stays there all those years later it brings back memories that sometimes, like the bath-time soapsuds, leave a stinging behind the eyes . . .

The Royal mother insisted that the upbringing of the children should be, as far as possible, like that of any normal if affluent family. The Duchess taught them about God, and the value of prayer, as well as reading them Bible tales. Sometimes the Prince of Wales, "Uncle David," called to take part in nursery games such as Snap, Happy Families and Racing Demon. A popular pastime was a game called Winnie-the-Pooh. The Duchess had read from the story book of that name, so David and his nieces enacted the characters in mime. She taught the girls to read via a literary diet of the Bible and fairy stories, such as *"Alice"*, *"Black Beauty"*, *"At the Back of the North Wind"*, *"Peter Pan"* — and anything about horses and dogs.

In their father's eyes, his daughters were both "wonderful and strange." Happy though that the sisters were in each other's company, they realised very early the restrictions placed upon them. Watching, at a distance, other children at play was to be reminded that others' lives were without red tape and ceremony, which is so much a part of a Royal existence.

Thrown inevitably together, the two Princesses, under the constant care of their mother, nurtured a strong bond of love and friendship. There was, occasionally, a certain amount of rivalry which ended in a fight. Such as when Margaret might pluck the elastic of her sister's hat, or when Elizabeth would pinch Margaret who would retaliate with a kick.

Basically, Princess Elizabeth was a sweet-natured child, but also capable of occasional rebellion; she once upturned an inkwell on her head to break the tedium of a French lesson. The less violent part of growing up took place in what must have been every little girl's dream — a child sized, two-storey thatched cottage in the grounds of the Lodge. It was a complete home scaled down in every detail — furniture, kitchen equipment, doors and windows and ceilings — to juvenile proportions, a gift from the people of Wales, so it was called *Y Bwthyn Bach Tô Gwellt* (The Little House with the Straw Roof).

Here the Princesses could play "houses" in a real house, which included inviting Mummy and Daddy for tea-parties served at a knee-high table just big enough for adults to squeeze their legs under. The Princesses could do make-believe chores, and their mother encouraged them to develop house-wifely skills in the cottage, though there was little chance that they would ever need them!

The Duchess was keen to send Elizabeth to school when she reached the age of seven, but the King put his foot down. She was Third in Line, and, though her accession did not seem very likely, Heirs to the Throne must always be educated at home. The answer was to appoint a Royal governess, who would eventually oversee the lessons of both Princesses and every aspect of the girls' upbringing. For this role the Duke and Duchess chose a young Scotswoman, Miss Marion Crawford. She had trained as a teacher in Edinburgh and intended to make her life's work among deprived children, but before settling down to her vocation she took a temporary job teaching the children of two families near her home at Dunfermline.

One of her employers was Lady Rose Leveson-Glower, sister to the Duchess of York, and it was through Lady Rose that the Duke and Duchess came to hear of her. In later years Miss Crawford, or "Crawfie" as she became known, was to upset the Royal Family because of her revelations about what went on behind the Palace gates. Much of the life of the young Princesses has come to light as a result of what she wrote.

On first meeting the Yorks, the Scots lassie found it "obvious that they were devoted to each other and very much in love."

According to Miss Crawford, "It was a couple of very spoiled and difficult people I somehow visualised as I travelled South, for already the papers had produced odd stories about these Royal children. I was more than convinced that my month's trial would stop at the end of the month, and that I should soon be home again." She stayed sixteen years.

Crawfie had Elizabeth from nine to six each day, but her out-of-school life remained in the care of "Alla" and the under-nurse, Margaret MacDonald, who shared a bedroom with the Princesses. When Crawfie arrived, Margaret was only two and not old enough for lessons.

Crawfie took to heart the Duke's worry that his daughters should have a lively childhood, and introduced them to gloriously grubby games of hide-and-seek. When in London they began to venture further afield into Hyde Park, but though the Princesses would gaze wistfully at the other children, they were not encouraged to make friends. Crawfie thought this was a pity, so she arranged dancing and swimming lessons to help them mix with other children.

While living in the centre of London, after the peace of Windsor, they became more conscious of being cut off from the bustling world outside. They would look out of the nursery windows at the top of the house to watch the buses rolling past and ask their governess about the real world beyond their home.

On Friday afternoons the family piled into a car and went down to Royal Lodge, where there was a lot to be done: a morning spent going over the previous week's lessons with Miss Crawford, followed by horse riding before lunch and then more riding or games in the garden or park with their parents. According to Crawfie, lunch was always taken with the Duke and Duchess whenever they were at home. Tea was occasionally taken with guests of their own age, but often with Uncle David.

The Duchess insisted that history and geography were more important than arithmetic as far as schooling was concerned. As a result young Elizabeth never did progress very far with mathematics, though intelligent and quick to learn in other subjects.

King George's educational demands were simpler: "For goodness' sake teach Margaret and Lilibet to write a decent hand, that's all I ask you. None of my children could write properly. They all do it exactly the same way. I like a hand with some character in it."

Although she never made friends again with her former charges after being so indiscreet with her writings in the late 1940s, Crawfie had only the fondest memories of her days with the Royals. She chronicled: "No one ever had employers who interfered so little. I often had the feeling that the Duke and Duchess, most happy in their own married life, were not over-concerned with the higher education of their daughters. They wanted most for them a really happy childhood, with lots of pleasant memories stored up against the days that might come and, later, happy marriages."

The Queen Mother ensured that Elizabeth and Margaret became accomplished in the social arts befitting Princesses. Singing and dancing came very easily to them. Elizabeth began riding at the age of four and by six had dispensed with the leading rein. Her teacher was the Duke's stud groom, Owen, who became such a hero to her that on one occasion her father remarked impatiently, "Don't ask me, ask Owen. Who am I to make suggestions?"

IN MAY 1935, King George V and Queen Mary celebrated the Silver Jubilee of their reign. The Yorks and their daughters joined in much of the public appearances that were part of the festivities. At that time the old Monarch was already clearly showing his favouritism for Bertie's wife and family. The King said to an old friend, Lady Algy Gordon-Lennox, "I pray to God that my eldest son will never marry and that nothing will come between Bertie and Lilibet and the Throne."

In the New Year of 1936, the King took to his bed at Sandringham and confessed to feeling "rotten" in his diary of Friday, 17th January. Most of the house guests disappeared, though the few who were left sat through a film which the King had ordered. The Duchess of York took the children out to walk in the light snow and explained that their grandfather was very ill.

On January 20th, 1936, King George V died, sooner than even his doctors had feared. Queen Mary rose to her feet at that moment and kissed the hand of her eldest son. At five minutes to midnight, David aged forty-one and carefree, was Edward VIII, the new King. He was to reign for 327 days and then abdicate.

Queen Mary recorded, "At five to twelve my darling husband passed peacefully away — my children were angelic." The body of George V lay in state for five days at Westminster Hall, and on the last night before his funeral his four sons stood watch at each corner of the catafalque. On a cold, gloomy morning six days later, the coffin was borne on a gun carriage to Paddington Station, then taken by train to Windsor where the funeral took place in St. George's Chapel. The new King remained a little apart from the rest of his family during the day's activities. No one knew then that uppermost in his mind was what he was going to do about Mrs. Wallis Simpson, the American divorcee with whom he was hopelessly in love: a King besotted with a commoner, who could never be his Queen.

The events of the next twelve months were to put the very future of the British Monarchy in jeopardy and change irrevocably the course of the Queen Mother's life.

His "playboy" world was not her world, but David was a welcome visitor who amused the two Princesses with his natural frivolity. He was always fun and he enjoyed being in a family atmosphere that he had never managed to create for himself.

Although the British public did not know of the rumours that were being printed abroad, Elizabeth and Bertie could see this trouble brewing from the start of David's relationship with the divorcee from Baltimore. They feared the final outcome because there could be no suggestion of a King marrying a divorced woman and remaining King. It was a hurtful time, in which the Duchess feared Bertie and herself and the children could come out the losers. By all accounts the Queen Mother did not approve of Mrs. Simpson and even today the whole business is something she will not discuss, even with her most intimate friends.

When her husband had to shoulder unexpected kingship, she had to lay aside the private life they both valued so much. She has always felt also that Bertie's life was shortened as a result of being burdened with the responsibilities laid upon him by the Abdication.

Soon after he became King, Edward VIII began to lose interest in the job, especially when he began to realise that it was the Government that was ruling the country, and not him. He did not bother to keep up with Cabinet papers and performed few public appearances. His entire life centred on Wallis Simpson.

MEANWHILE, THE DUKE and Duchess of York and the rest of the family developed that very British trait of behaving in an impeccably polite but frosty manner when Bertie brought that woman into their company.

Now that brother David was King, though uncrowned, everyone hoped he would see sense and drop the American woman. Optimistically, Prime Minister Stanley Baldwin said at the time of the accession: ". . . he has the secret of youth in the prime of age; he has a wider and more intimate knowledge of all classes of his subjects, not only at home, but throughout the Dominions and India, than any of his predecessors . . . We look forward with confidence and assurance to the new reign."

He underestimated the influence of Mrs. Wallis Simpson. The late King had no illusions, for he is reputed to have told Baldwin: "After I am gone, the boy will ruin himself in twelve months."

Wallis was granted her second divorce — to Ernest Simpson — discreetly at Ipswich on October 27th, 1936. But when the public got to know of it the storm broke. While Elizabeth and Bertie waited anxiously the King had to make one of three choices: Defy his Ministers, marry the woman he loved and bring about a monumental crisis; have a morganatic marriage, whereby she would be his wife, but not his Queen, and their children would have no position in the Line of Succession; or renounce Mrs. Simpson.

Edward VIII struggled in a battle for several months with his Ministers, his sense of duty to his country — and to the woman he loved. When she watched the TV series "*Edward and Mrs. Simpson*" the Queen Mother must have been painfully reminded of the torture she and her husband's family were going through at the time. For them it was not mere video drama between commercial breaks, but a series of brittle clashes between son and father — brother against brother.

THE AGONIES of waiting by the Duke and Duchess of York did not go unnoticed by the love-lorn King. Edward, by then the Duke of Windsor, acknowledged their bewilderment in his memoirs. "Bertie had most at stake: it was he who would have to wear the Crown if I left, and his genuine concern for me was mixed up with the dread of having to assume the responsibilities of Kingship."

But Edward wanted to have his monarchial cake and eat it, keeping the Throne and Mrs. Simpson. "I cannot with full heart carry out my duties in the loneliness that surrounds me," he said. He seemed to be beyond control. As uncrowned King Edward VIII, he felt he had even more freedom to carry on his affair. To critics he would protest: "I am the King, after all."

He ensconced Wallis in Fort Belvedere, his private house near Windsor, and she would always be there waiting for him at the end of his days of official duties. He showered her with jewellery, including some diamonds from the family vaults that were considered Royal heirlooms. She was said to be "dripping in new jewels and clothes."

Edward further upset Elizabeth and Bertie when, while the Court was still in mourning after the death of George VI, he abandoned public engagements in Aberdeen, including a visit to a hospital, to be with Wallis, who had been sneaked into nearby Balmoral.

The nation faced a turning point in the history of the Monarchy and Elizabeth watched anxiously, knowing all too well how her own life could change in a direction she never wanted.

The possibility of a morganatic marriage was floated by some of Edward's political friends, and Stanley Baldwin put the suggestion to his Cabinet, who gave it a resounding thumbs-down. As pressure built up, Wallis went to the South of France, where she said she would be willing to give up the King and end their affair, but Edward would not hear of it. He always hoped that one day she would be accepted as his wife while he still retained the Crown.

But those around the Court refused to accept such an idea.

Eventually he came to his shattering decision. He told Prime Minister Baldwin: "I want you to be the first to know I have made my mind up and nothing will alter it. I mean to abdicate and marry Mrs. Simpson."

During the final hours of decision-making Elizabeth was in bed with influenza. When news came that she was to be Queen she said to her children's governess, "I am afraid there are going to be great changes in our life, Crawfie . . . we must take what is coming to us, and make the best of it."

The nation faced a turning point in the history of the Monarchy and Elizabeth watched anxiously, knowing all too well how her own life could change in a direction she never wanted.

THE DAY THAT CHANGED HER LIFE

ON A RAINY Friday evening, December 11th, 1936, Elizabeth listened with horror to the uncrowned King's Abdication broadcast. Every word hammered home the desperate future ahead. He said:

"A few hours ago I discharged my last duty as King and Emperor, and now that I have been succeeded by my brother, the Duke of York, my first words must be to declare my allegiance to him. This I do with all my heart.

"You all know the reasons that have impelled me to renounce the Throne. But I want you to understand that in making up my mind I did not forget the country or the Empire which, as Prince of Wales and lately as King, I have for twenty-five years tried to serve. But you must believe me when I tell you that I have found it impossible to carry the heavy burden of responsibility and to discharge my duties as King as I would wish to do without the help and support of the woman I love.

"The Ministers of the Crown, and in particular Mr. Baldwin, the Prime Minister, have always treated me with full consideration. There has never been any constitutional difference between me and them and between me and Parliament. Bred in the constitutional tradition by my father, I should never have allowed any such issue to arise . . .

"I now quit altogether public affairs, and I lay down my burden. It may be some time before I return to my native land, but I shall always follow the fortunes of the British race and Empire with profound interest, and if at any time in the future I can be found of

service to His Majesty in a private station I shall not fail.

"And now we all have a new King. I wish him, and you, his people, happiness and prosperity with all my heart. God Bless you all. God Save the King."

Then stripped of his titles except the one created for the occasion, "His Royal Highness the Duke of Windsor," Edward bid farewell to his brother and sailed to exile in France. Six months later, on 3rd June, 1937 he and Wallis were married at the Chateau de Cande, near Tours.

By that time the new Queen Elizabeth could see the strain of monarchy was showing on her husband.

"Bertie was so much taken aback by my news that in his shy way he could not bring himself to express his innermost feelings at the time," Edward, when 'demoted' to the Duke of Windsor, recalled in his memoirs later. Bertie spent the next ten days pleading with his elder brother to see sense, without success.

When his brother abdicated, Bertie was appalled. "This can't be happening to me," he protested when a servant correctly addressed him as "Your Majesty". He said miserably to Lord Mountbatten, "This is terrible, Dickie, I never wanted this to happen. I'm quite unprepared for it . . . I've never seen a State paper. I'm only a Naval officer. It's the only thing I known about." He wept in front of his mother.

George V had always regarded Bertie as a second fiddle, denying him access to State papers, considering them to be none of his business. It had never been expected that he would be King, so he was never provided with the special education and grooming for Monarchy.

When, earlier this year, a book was published of the private correspondence between the Duke and Duchess of Windsor, the Queen Mother was hurt by criticism about her relationship with her brother-in-law and the two-time divorcee who caused his Abdication.

The Queen Mother told her closest friends that she was adamant that there was never a "Royal feud" between her and Wallis Simpson, and that she was "distressed" at being portrayed as an "ogre" in books written about the situation.

She was keen for it to be known that she had no involvement whatsoever in King Edward VIII's Abdication and that it was entirely a "political matter." She also said she was "very hurt" at the portrayal of her conducting a vendetta against the Duchess.

She insisted she did not know Wallis well and that it was the Duchess who sought to create an imaginary hostility, to gain sympathy in the eyes of the world. But, despite her protests, of all the Royal Family, the Queen Mother is the only one living who remembers every detail of the Abdication and the scandalous months leading up to it.

She can never forget that while her brother-in-law didn't really want to be King, her husband certainly didn't. But whereas Edward VIII just gave in, George VI stuck with it. In all the years that passed since the Abdication to Mrs. Simpson's death, the Queen Mother only spoke to her once. That was when the Duchess of Windsor attended her husband's funeral. The Queen Mother, somehow overriding the half-century of bitterness bottled inside her took her arm and said: "I know how you feel, I've been through it, too."

Those were about the only kind words she had for the American divorcee. For their feelings go far, far back, and go deep.

Mrs. Simpson used to refer to the Queen Mother, then Duchess of York, as "the dowdy duchess" or sometimes, on bad-tempered days, as "that 14-carat beauty."

Then came the dawning realisation that she would never be Queen. And the knife went in deeper. The lady who today is a byword for graciousness and good manners, was dubbed "the monster of Glamis."

The feud had begun at the first meeting between the Scottish Earl's daughter and the brash divorcee from Baltimore in the early 1930s. Elizabeth made it plain that she would

never accept this woman she considered over-dressed, over made-up and over-ambitious.

Wallis was only too aware of the icy opposition from her comparatively quaintly-dressed future sister-in-law. Daggers were drawn every time they met. Never more so than one night in September, 1936, at Balmoral during Edward's short reign.

Anger must have been raging in Elizabeth knowing that Wallis was playing hostess alongside the King and even sleeping in Queen Mary's bed. When Elizabeth arrived at the Castle for dinner, she warmly smiled at Edward and ignored Wallis saying: "I came to dine with the King." Within three months Edward had abdicated and the enmity between the two women became intense.

The Duchess's bitterness was over the title "Her Royal Highness" which George VI never conferred on her. She was convinced Queen Elizabeth influenced him to refuse it. One week before the Windsors' wedding the King exercised his prerogative and an announcement in the London Gazette proclaimed the ex-King was to be HRH. But not Wallis.

She would be simply Her Grace the Duchess of Windsor, and therefore not entitled to be addressed as "Ma'am."

The Queen Mother has shouldered the entire burden of blame for this act of family censure which thwarted the Duke's dearest wish, yet this is not completely true.

King George V had made up his mind that Wallis Simpson could never be a Royal Highness at least two years before his eldest son abdicated.

Unknown to the Prince of Wales, the old King had prepared a dossier on a little-known part of the life of the woman Queen Mary referred to scathingly as "an adventuress."

King George V disliked her and feared her power over his son. Queen Mary said she would never receive her.

So although the Queen Mother has had to bear all the blame on her own shoulders and has been identified as the principal opposition, she was not alone.

In her own memoirs, the Duchess of Windsor recalled some of the few meetings between her and her sister-in-law. One was in the Spring of 1936 after Edward had succeeded to the Throne. The new King had bought an American-style station wagon and insisted on driving it over to Royal Lodge in Windsor Great Park to show it to his younger brother, Bertie.

Wallis went with him.

"Her justly famous charm was highly evident," Wallis wrote. "I was also aware of the beauty of her complexion and the almost startling blueness of her eyes. Our conversation, I remember, was largely a discussion of the merits of the garden at the Fort and at Royal Lodge.

"It was a pleasant hour. But I left with a distinct impression that while the Duke of York was sold on the American station wagon, the Duchess was not sold on David's other American interest."

The two women were to meet again thirty years later in June 1967. The occasion was the unveiling of a plaque to Queen Mary, who had died fourteen years earlier. The Queen Mother, entitled to a bow or curtsey from all but the Reigning Monarch and her husband, walked over to where the Windsors were standing. The Duke bent his head in a courtly bow. The Duchess shook her hand. They did not kiss. She did not curtsey.

Signs of fifty years of bitterness between the Royal Family and the Duchess of Windsor lingered on even up to the day her coffin was placed overnight after being flown from Paris in April 1986. The Queen and other Royals paid their respects beside the Duchess's oak coffin in the Albert Memorial Chapel at Windsor Castle. But the Queen Mother was not among the mourners.

She spent part of the day at Royal Lodge and was later driven to Clarence House. Her Press secretary, Major John Griffin, said: "She did not visit the castle. She will pay her respects at the funeral."

In another snub the Duchess was buried alongside her husband, still without the Royal title that eluded her all her life. Neither the inscription on her coffin, nor the memorial tablet placed later in the Royal Family's private burial ground at Frogmore, Windsor, carried the style and title HRH. The funeral was a private family affair in contrast to the full state ceremony for the Duke of Windsor when he was buried there fourteen years earlier.

Over the years the Queen had tried to persuade her mother to let bygones be bygones. But the bitter feelings that prevented the Queen Mother from relenting revealed the uncompromising, strong-willed side of a woman admired by a nation for her graceful charm. She refused to bury the hatchet even while the Duchess was chronically sick.

But all that was in the future. When the King abdicated there was not so much a change, more an upheaval. An indication of that came after Bertie and his wife returned from the public proclamation as King George VI.

Elizabeth, now uncrowned Queen, together with her husband and children left 145 Piccadilly for ever for a new life at Buckingham Palace.

The Royal Apartments were on the first floor, overlooking Green Park in one direction and the garden in the other. On the floor above were the nurseries. Here the Princesses lived, high enough to see over the Victoria Memorial and along the Mall; a perfect spot for viewing the Changing of the Guard each morning in the forecourt below. Elizabeth and her girls excitedly, and noisily, explored the long corridors. "It was as though the place had been dead for years and had suddenly come alive," said a member of staff.

In normal circumstances a year to eighteen months separates a Sovereign's Accession and Coronation, but the arrangements for Edward VIII's crowning were adhered to. Wednesday, May 12th, 1937 had already been set for the — now urgent — Coronation of a new Sovereign.

No one at Buckingham Palace was able to sleep much on the eve of the Coronation. Bertie and Elizabeth were awake by three o'clock in the morning, and the new King was so nervous that he could not eat breakfast.

The Accession of the King, at 41, was not only a shock for the new Monarch but it affected his wife and daughters' lives also. "Nothing in the Abdication cut so deep as the changed future for their children; it was hardest of all for their sake," said Queen Elizabeth's brother, Sir David Bowes-Lyon.

In his farewell broadcast Edward VIII had said of his brother: "He has one matchless blessing, enjoyed by so many of you and not bestowed on me — a happy home with his wife and children." Happy, yes, but an entirely different atmosphere was now surrounding Elizabeth and Bertie's family.

It was an atmosphere that could have suffocated George but for Elizabeth. Those close to him believed he could not have done the job without her support. He himself acknowledged this in his first New Year's message to the Empire and the Commonwealth when he said he shouldered his new responsibilities "with all the more confidence in the knowledge that the Queen and my mother Queen Mary are at my side." Mary, that rock on whom lesser Royals have foundered, had to take second place. His faith in his wife was well-founded and one his aged mother dare not take issue with: such was the power and personality of Elizabeth.

He also paid full tribute to her in another broadcast: "With my wife and helpmeet by my side, I take up the heavy task which lies before me."

If ever a lack-lustre, shy and nervous princeling turned reluctant king needed the help of a strong woman, it was now. His speech impediment, delicate health and general lack of confidence were liabilities that did little to encourage his subjects. Many thought that he would be just a rubberstamp king. Elizabeth knew that it was vital that she should back her husband up to the hilt to restore confidence in a shaken Monarchy and nation.

She was firmly convinced that she could do the job, she felt the British people would be behind her . . . and so she set out to sustain the new King, through thick and thin. But more, much more than that was needed, and she did not shirk what by now she clearly perceived to be her duty and one destined to echo down the century.

She accompanied him on public engagements and official tours. Her support became legendary. Her loving advice and utter belief in him enabled the King to come to terms, first of all with that stammer which plagued his speeches, and then the early nightmares of personal appearances. This meant Elizabeth continuing to spend hours at home with him, patiently building up his confidence.

It is a tribute to her courage that she changed from an unambitious duchess to the determined wife of the Reigning Monarch in a matter of days. By the time they went on their first State visit to Paris early in 1938, Elizabeth was firmly set in her role. So much so that the French were completely won over, although she herself, knowing the French, modestly attributed much of this to the wardrobe Norman Hartnell created specially for her. His billowy dresses and large hats laid the foundations of a style which today is still known as "Queen Motherish."

As the early years of Kingship progressed, George became more sure of himself. He found with some surprise that interest and affection were directed towards him as well as towards the Queen. Elizabeth had always seemed to be taking the lead, instinctively knowing how to approach strangers and put them at their ease. But now a subtle change was creeping in. The King finally found confidence in himself and — for once — was able to give support to his wife.

NO ONE WAS happier than Elizabeth to see how things were developing. She was so proud of her husband, and the way he had measured up to his responsibilities. It would be hard to find in British history a consort who equalled her achievements in being a "helpmeet" or one who achieved such popular esteem and private worth.

But she still had her doubts. Elizabeth once asked Ramsay MacDonald, the Scots politician, a few months after she became Queen: "Am I doing all right?" She was. Not only as Queen but also as a mother, because in addition that was another role she was anxious to fill to the full. And there was a lot to be done in that direction.

With the excitement of a Coronation over, Elizabeth and her daughters settled down to a bewildering new routine of living in a huge house, at the centre of global attention, and as a parent who no longer had as much time to spare for her family. King George and Queen Elizabeth were anxious, though, that their daughters should not be cut off from the real world.

Children from outside the Royal Circle

were allowed into the Palace. A Buckingham Palace Girl Guide company and Brownie pack were formed. Princess Elizabeth joined the Kingfisher Patrol of the Girl Guides, and Princess Margaret joined the Leprechaun Six of the Brownies. They continued guide activities at Windsor during the Second World War, and were joined by cockney evacuees to the Royal Estate.

The new Queen noticed with regret that Elizabeth, the young teenager who was never destined for the Throne from birth, had to find a new life, taking on a more serious aspect, because she had to be trained to become Sovereign. Private lessons became more purposeful, and a little of the girl's lightheartedness disappeared as she became more involved in protocol and learning about the Affairs of State.

The Heir — or Heiress — to the Throne, described by the *Daily Telegraph* as "Everybody's Daughter," had a forbidding curriculum. Languages, history, economics and deportment were just a few subjects. French, German and Latin were essential for anyone who had to understand the workings of British law and constitution. The King and Queen helped her in her languages by speaking to her at "French lunches" — gatherings at table where not one word of English was uttered: vital for someone who would one day be the ruler of French-speaking Canada. It was also invaluable as the main second language.

The Queen and Bertie also arranged that, as she got older, Princess Elizabeth received special tutoring in constitutional history from Sir Henry Marten, the Vice-Provost of Eton College.

As the Princesses grew older, Queen Elizabeth had to cope with the usual chores of every other mother: helping them with their homework . . . making sure they behaved properly outside the home . . . choosing clothes and taking them to parties . . . and the early confusion of being teenagers. All of these duties were more difficult because the family was so much in the public eye.

However, in the closing years of the 1930s, the threat of another war was constantly in the background. At the beginning of August 1939, the Royal Family had gone to its annual Highland holiday at Balmoral.

WAR AND PEACE!

ON SEPTEMBER 3rd, 1939, Britain declared war on Germany. King George and Queen Elizabeth hastened back to London, leaving Elizabeth and Margaret in what they hoped would be peaceful Scotland.

As horrific as it was and as great was the suffering of the British people during the Second World War, it resulted not just in victory but gave a tremendous boost to the reputation of the Monarchy. After the Windsor debacle, Royalty needed help, and it was during those dark six years from 1939 to 1945 that the people's loyalty to the Crown was re-established . . . a loyalty that our present Queen benefits from to this day.

By the time war broke out most parents with money or influence were getting their children out of the cities or even out of the country altogether — to America, Canada and Australia. King George and Queen Elizabeth decided to set an example to the rest of Britain by staying as a family at home in the United Kingdom.

With his stammer and nervous air, George did not come across as a natural "warrior King." But he was a brave man nevertheless and, as Sovereign, completely dedicated. The King himself was fully prepared to lead a resistance movement if England had been invaded.

The first Christmas of the war was spent at Sandringham, despite its proximity to one of the stretches of coast thought most likely to be invaded. It was his wife, who helped King George VI prepare a stirring message to the Empire in the traditional Christmas broadcast. After calling for a girding of the loins and recognition of the dangers facing his people, he ended with a poem that stayed and stays in the memory, even now, of those who recall those days . . .

It was "The Gate of the Year", written by Marie Louise Haskins, a lecturer at the London School of Economics.

*I said to the man who stood at the Gate of
   the Year,
"Give me a light so that I may tread safely
   into the unknown,"
And he replied, "Go out into the darkness,
And put your hand into the Hand of God.
That shall be to you better than light,
And safer than a known way."*

Princess Elizabeth and Princess Margaret stayed at Sandringham until February 1940, when they moved to Windsor Castle. Windsor was beneath the flight path of German aircraft following the Thames to London, and in time the Princesses could identify the bombers by the sounds they made. The castle's hundreds of windows were protected, as far as possible, by "stuck-on" mesh, overlaid with wire-netting, and, at night, lost behind thick, black out curtaining.

The technology of "blitzkrieg" meant that it was no longer the impenetrable fortress once thought, but it still had greater facilities for the Royal Family's safety than Royal Lodge. Indeed, the castle, on the banks of the Thames, soon became the wartime home of Queen Elizabeth, her husband and daughters. And a plan was devised to snatch them to safety should the need arise.

If there had been a Nazi landing, a refuge had been devised in strictest secrecy. A bodyguard chosen from the Brigade of Guards and the Household Cavalry was charged with their care. Four houses in different areas were stocked with all the requirements for an emergency, and armoured cars, specially marked to ensure priority, stood by to speed them into hiding — and safety.

The pattern laid down was that Buckingham Palace was the daytime base of George and Elizabeth, and Windsor Castle the home to which they returned to spend evenings with the children. The King and Queen were always back at the Palace by daylight. It was bombed twice . . . once on the night of September 10th, 1940, and again two days later during a daring daylight raid, when they had a narrow escape. It happened when a German bomber flew straight up the Mall to drop two sticks of six bombs each on Buckingham Palace. Two of the bombs exploded in the quadrangle below the windows of a room they were occupying.

The King and Queen had been working together in their room when, as he wrote afterwards, "All of a sudden we heard an aircraft making a zooming noise above us. Saw two bombs falling past the opposite side of the Palace and then heard two resounding crashes as the bombs fell in the quadrangle about thirty yards away. We looked at each other and then we were out in the passage as fast as we could get there . . . we all wondered why we weren't dead. . ."

A basement room in Buckingham Palace was converted into an air-raid shelter, although the style was not exactly that of most back-garden dug-outs. For a start, most back-garden dug-outs weren't furnished with Regency chairs, a settee, and hunting-shooting-fishing and society magazines which were replaced regularly by servants. In all, bombs fell six times on Royal homes during the war, including 145 Piccadilly. It was completely destroyed.

When, in the late summer of 1940, invasion seemed imminent, there was increased pressure from the Government, led by Winston Churchill, for Princesses Elizabeth and Margaret to be sent to Canada, both for safety and to protect the Royal Line. The Queen would have none of it: "The children cannot go without me, and I cannot possibly leave the King," she reposted icily. Then calmly proceeded to take up revolver training. This was just another example of the backbone she demonstrated. At her insistence the family, whenever possible, shared in the deprivation suffered by their subjects. Their clothing was limited to the allowance dictated by strict rationing, making do with what they had collected before the war . . . frequently patched up over the six years.

Heating in the Palace was cut to minimal. Extra warm woollies had to do, while just a tiny electric fire would heat bedrooms. To save fuel again, there was a line painted above the plug-holes in baths to mark the hot water mark.

Meals, too, were the same as everyone else getting by on rationing. But nevertheless standards were standards and the mainly meatless sausages and powdered eggs were solemnly served up on gold and silver dishes.

Night after night in those terrible months of 1940, Nazi bombers hammered the East End of London, killing and maiming thousands of men, women and children. Life seemed to be a permanent existence underground in cellars and air-raid shelters, or on the platforms of Tube stations.

Although we have heard of many tales of bravery and courage in those days, since then it has also come to light that the War Cabinet began to be worried about the cracking up of morale among the workers who were being blasted by bombers. Some secret reports talked of plans by groups of East Enders to march on the West End of London and attack the homes of the mainly unscathed rich in the smart areas around Buckingham Palace.

IT WAS SO bad that when, eventually the Palace was bombed, the Queen Mother told her husband; "I'm glad we've been bombed. It makes me feel I can look the East End in the face."

And look it straight in the eye she did when, at the urging of the War Cabinet, she and George VI visited the bombed areas in London and elsewhere in Britain.

Their presence amid the ruins had a considerable effect on raising people's spirits during those dark days. As one Cockney bomb victim put it; "She came with courage in her eyes, and when she left, she left some of it with you. Suddenly you felt like carrying on when you hadn't before."

Churchill, never at a loss for the right words, was more colourful, of course; "Many an aching heart found solace in her gracious smile."

Among the foreign royals who fled to Britain after the Nazi invasion of Northern Europe and stayed with the British Royals was Queen Wilhelmina of the Netherlands. She brought with her the future Queen Juliana and grand-daughters Beatrix and Irene. And so a friendship was struck between the British Royal Family and the Dutch monarchy that is still

strong all these years later.

Although perhaps leading a more sheltered existence than most, there were other reminders of the struggle beyond Palace walls. Elizabeth made arrangements for the Princesses to meet evacuee children from the Glasgow slums when they were accommodated on the Royal Estate at Balmoral. And when the menacing voice of William Joyce, better known as "Lord Haw-Haw", Hitler's anti-British propaganda "star," was heard on the radio, Lilibet and Margaret would throw books, cushions and any other handy missiles at the set.

During the first Christmas at Windsor, in December 1940, Elizabeth arranged for the Princesses and local evacuees to act in a nativity play, which was so successful that their ambitions rose to a pantomime. With the help of a master and pupils from the Royal School at Windsor Great Park, they performed *Cinderella*. Their stage was the one erected by Queen Victoria in the Waterloo Room for earlier family theatricals. The King was thrilled by their confidence: "I don't know how they do it," he said. "We were always so terribly shy and self-conscious as children. These two don't seem to care."

The family's love of theatricals was given further outlet on subsequent Christmases with performances of *The Sleeping Beauty* in 1942, *Aladdin* — in which young cousins, the Duke of Kent and Princess Alexandra, were also cast — in 1943, and *Old Mother Red Riding Boots* in 1944. A further outlet for Royal talents was the Royal Windsor Society, which included among its enthusiasts young Guards officers and boys from Eton public school.

As young Elizabeth got older her mother introduced her to selected teenage boys and young men of the right background. There was the practice, for example, of inviting two Guards officers to join the family for lunch every day at Windsor.

The Royal Family emerged from the war years with its reputation revitalised to become the institution that is so respected and loved today. Churchill was able to write to George after victory was won: "This war has drawn the Throne and the people more closely together than was ever before recorded, and Your Majesties are more beloved by all classes and conditions than any of the princes of the past."

In no small measure, credit for that was due to his Queen, beloved wife of "Bertie."

When the Royal Family looked around them after the war they found that inside the Palace carpets were threadbare and patched, while outside Britain bore the scars of war. After the euphoria of national celebrations came the struggle to get the country back on its feet. And so the soldiers, the sailors and the airmen returned. Among them one Lieutenant Prince Philip of Greece. His arrival had a remarkable effect on the young Princess Elizabeth.

She had taken to playing over and over again on the gramophone the "*Oklahoma*" hit, "*People will say we're in love . . .*" and on a desk in her room for more than a year was a photograph of a fair-haired sailor, recently replaced by a new one in which the face was hidden behind a bushy beard that made him almost totally unrecognisable. To all, that is, except Princess Elizabeth.

Her romance with Philip was so delightfully uncomplicated that it was almost out of a fairy tale, compared to sister Margaret's turbulent relationships. When Elizabeth showed an interest in this young Naval chap who was a protégé of his uncle, Lord Louis Mountbatten, her mother saw the signs as long ago as the pre-war days when Philip had met her daughter at Dartmouth Naval College in Devon.

Philip and Elizabeth had met before, but never really caught one another's eye until then. They had been together briefly at the same Royal functions — the marriage of Philip's cousin, Princess Marina, to the Duke of Kent, for example, and the Coronation. The difference in ages was too great for them to have taken any real notice of each other, however. At the time of her father's Coronation, Princess Elizabeth was only eleven, while he was sixteen and already a young man.

Lord Mountbatten was in attendance as the King's ADC on the day of the visit to the Naval college, so it seemed natural that another Royal relative, Philip, should be appointed Captain's doggie (messenger) for the day. There was a special service in the college chapel, which Elizabeth and Margaret would normally have attended with their parents, but because some of the college cadets had developed mumps, it was felt wiser for the girls to stay away. Instead they went along to the Captain's (Sir Frederick Hew George Dalrymple-Hamilton) house to play with the Dalrymple-Hamilton children, a slightly older boy and girl.

The slim, ash-blond Philip joined them, helping the younger children operate a toy train set, munching biscuits with them, drinking lemonade. He showed the Princesses the college swimming-pool and also played croquet with them. When the Royal Yacht set sail again, the college cadets piled into a variety of small craft to escort it out to sea.

Some followed it too far. They were signalled to turn back. All except one did so. The exception was Philip. He continued to pull at the oars of the small boat he was rowing. Elizabeth watched him through binoculars, taking a long, final glimpse at the young man she had begun to set her heart on.

The Queen Mother soon noticed that her eldest daughter had developed a teenage crush on this man, who was her third cousin through their joint links created generations earlier by Queen Victoria.

Two years later Princess Elizabeth and Prince Philip had a second meeting at Buckingham Palace, and they kept up a steady correspondence during the war, when he was serving on destroyers. Often he used to spend his leave at Windsor Castle, and there was one pantomime when Princess Elizabeth cared very much how well she acted, for Philip was sitting in the front row.

The Queen Mother, not being quite sure of her husband's reaction, knew what was going on and decided to allow matters to run their natural course. All she ever wanted was her daughter's happiness. When it dawned on the King that his daughter — by now seventeen — was interested in Lord Louis' nephew, he argued that Elizabeth was too young and too inexperienced to think of marriage. Just like any other father. He told Queen Mary in 1944: "We both think she is too young for that now, as she has never met any young man of her own age. I like Philip. He is intelligent, has a good sense of humour and thinks about things in the right way."

Then there was the sting in the tail: "Philip had better not think any more about it for the present."

Despite this early fatherly opposition, mother Elizabeth thought she had better take a hand, and when the war was over, Philip was among the first guests at Balmoral and Buckingham Palace. He became a frequent visitor, encouraged by his future mother-in-law's enthusiasm. Whenever he could get leave from his Naval duties he would be there, even though the King wanted Elizabeth to meet more men, so that at every opportunity eligible suitors were introduced into her company. They never stood a chance. The Queen Mother, with an eye for romance, was delighted to see this.

PHILIP WAS given a shore job by the Navy and became much more accessible to Elizabeth. The King played his last card when he asked his wife to arrange grand balls at the Palace so that Elizabeth could meet a wide range of young men. He did not look forward to losing his daughter so soon after he was, at last, able to spend more time with her than the early years of Kingship and the war had allowed.

Elizabeth was independent of mind and strong of will, though — and in love. Philip formally proposed to her in the summer of 1946. She first accepted him, and only then went off to tell her parents. The King did not raise any more objections but insisted on delaying any announcement.

Philip and Elizabeth were parted when the two Princesses went with their parents on a tour of South Africa in 1947. The Queen Mother noticed that her elder daughter was quiet and subdued when she was told about the African trip.

A visit to the then Dominion of South Africa had first been proposed by the South African leader, General Smuts, a year or two earlier. Now there were strong feelings of republicanism in the country, with calls among the Afrikaaners for secession from Britain. A visit by the King and Queen, together with their daughters, was looked upon as a method of healing the rifts with the British Crown.

At one point in the tour the Queen Mother was told by a veteran of the Boer War, "Pleased to have met you, Ma'am, but we still feel sometimes that we cannot forgive the English . . ." "I understand perfectly," she replied. "We feel very much the same in Scotland, too."

The Royal Family sailed in the Navy's newest battleship, *Vanguard*, which Princess Elizabeth had launched two years previously.

It was on January 31st when they left Portsmouth on what was to be the last overseas tour of George VI's reign. Their departure coincided with the worst British winter within living memory. Ice, snow, gales and fog paralysed the country. Within four days, two million people had been thrown out of work by a chronic coal shortage. Food ships were held up in dock and supply trains halted by snowfalls.

As the Royal Party sailed into the sun, young Elizabeth wrote in her diary, "While we are scorching, we feel rather guilty at being right away from it all." When *Vanguard* arrived at Cape Town, a reporter for the African channel on local radio is reputed to have described the Royal quartet as "The King and the Queen and the fruit of their loins, Elizabeth and Margaret."

King George and his family travelled ten thousand miles by car or train in two months. There was a succession of receptions, inspections, official dinners, parties . . . rest days were few and far between. It was a tough schedule of functions, meetings with tribes and their chiefs, inspections of military units, visits to national shrines and natural beauty spots.

It was noticed by members of the entourage that Princess Elizabeth seemed to be quiet, even moody at times. This was put down to the forbidden subject — Philip back home.

The tension between the opposing political factions and between the races was such that, during the tour, the harassed King-Emperor several times showed irritation and temper in public.

There was even a spot of black comedy. While driving through the Reef towns in an open Daimler limousine one day, a huge Zulu burst from the crowd and rushed towards the slow-moving car, shouting with apparent ferocity. His fingers clutched the car and he hung on with something in his free hand while the Queen beat him off with her parasol until it broke in two.

The police knocked him down, thinking they were dealing with a potential assassin. In fact he was clutching a ten-shilling note loyally intended as a birthday gift for Princess Elizabeth.

From South Africa the Royal Family went to Rhodesia, now Zimbabwe. Near Bulawayo the party walked up the granite hill slope to the grave of Cecil Rhodes until the Queen found she could not move another step in her high-heeled shoes. Princess Elizabeth lent her mother her own sandals and continued to climb in her stockinged feet. "It was so like Mummy to set out in those shoes," said the Princess.

The separation in South Africa did not kill the romance, and when the Royal Family returned to Britain, George, at his wife's behest, had to accept that Philip and Elizabeth were very much in love.

So it was that the official Court Circular of Wednesday, July 9th, 1947 contained these words: "It is with great pleasure that the King and Queen announce the betrothal of their dearly beloved daughter, the Princess Elizabeth, to Lieutenant Philip Mountbatten, RN, son of the late Prince Andrew, to which union the King has gladly given his consent."

PRINCESS ELIZABETH was twenty-one, her fiancé twenty-six. The news that the King had told Elizabeth that she could marry her sailor brought the first post-war cheer to a glum world in 1947.

After announcing the engagement, King George VI mused: "He's the right man for the job, but I wonder if he knows what he's taking on. One day Lilibet will be Queen and he will be Consort. And that's much harder than being a king." The King had just under six years to live — Philip's role in the Monarchy, with all its problems, was much nearer than anyone imagined!

A date was set — Thursday, November 20th, 1947. It would be the first wedding in English history of an Heiress Presumptive who would one day become Queen.

Bearing in mind that the Government was against a "big splash," King George VI and Queen Elizabeth decided that there should be no lavish display. They also decided that George would pay from his own Privy Purse all the wedding expenses, apart from street decorations in Whitehall and the Mall. In addition he would cover the expenses of the newly-weds for two years.

Thought had been given to a private, quiet wedding in St. George's Chapel at Windsor, but more extravagant heads among the Royal advisers decided to be daring and choose Westminster Abbey — the traditional venue for the crowning and marrying of monarchs.

So the scene was set. The day of the wedding was grey but mild. The Mall was lined with thirty-two tall poles, hung with yellow and white banners bearing "E" in gold and red medallions. And the crowd. The crowd was enormous. Nothing like it had been seen in London since the Coronation ten years previously. It was happy and good-tempered, thousands upon thousands of people who were determined to enjoy a brief respite from the harsh, hard, austerity of the past few years. Flags and streamers flowered from every other hand. It seemed that all the colour and gaiety and happiness the world had to offer was concentrated on that day . . . and no one was happier than the mother of the bride.

Hard days they may have been, with rationing restrictions and the ugly scars of war still evident, but, according to the writings of Lady Airlie, Queen Mary's lady-in-waiting, there was "a week of gaiety such as the Court had not seen for years. There were parties at St. James's Palace to view the wedding presents, a Royal dinner party for all the foreign royalties, and an evening party at Buckingham Palace which seemed, after the years of austerity, like a scene out of a fairy tale."

What a fairy tale, and what a part the Queen, today our Queen Mother, had to play. No one, in truth, knows just what she had to say to the King, but on the eve of the wedding he invited Philip to give up his Greek title as a prince and honoured him with British titles. He was created a Royal Highness, Baron Greenwich, Earl of Merioneth and Duke of Edinburgh. "It is a great deal to give a man all at once, but I know Philip understands his new responsibilities on his marriage to Lilibet," said George.

Wartime clothes rationing was still in force, so Queen Elizabeth arranged a collection among relatives of a hundred clothing coupons needed to make the Princess's gown. Another twenty-five each were allotted to her bridesmaids. George VI told his daughter later, that when he escorted her to the altar: "I was so proud of you and thrilled at having you so close to me on our long walk in Westminster Abbey, but when I handed your hand to the Archbishop I felt that I had lost something very precious. You were so calm and composed during the service and said your words with such conviction." This was the King who, at one time, suffered from a lack of conviction in himself . . . until, that is, he married the Lady Elizabeth Glamis.

PRINCESS ELIZABETH sent a letter from her Scottish honeymoon to her parents thanking them for all they had done. But the King had a letter of his own to write: "Your leaving us has left a great blank in our lives, but do remember that your old home is still yours and do come back to it as much and as often as possible. I can see that you are sublimely happy with Philip, which is right, but don't forget us. This is the wish of your ever-loving and devoted Papa."

He also wrote: "Our family, us four, the 'Royal Family', must remain together, with additions, of course, at suitable moments. I have watched you grow up all these years with pride under the skilful direction of Mummy, who, as you know, is the most marvellous person in the world in my eyes, and I can, I know, always count on you, and now Philip, to help us in our work."

No wonder he thought her marvellous. The debt the Royal Family owes the Queen Mother to this day is incalculable. Behind that smile and soft mouth is a will of steel.

Marrying Princess Elizabeth brought Philip a stable family life for the first time. Until then he had been virtually a nomad, living with relations throughout Europe, and a solitary Naval officer who had never really known a permanent home. It also brought Queen Elizabeth and King George a grandson. But the joy was to be tempered with worry . . . it seemed, almost, that Queen Elizabeth's strength was always to be tested. In the last few weeks of his daughter's pregnancy George — the heavy smoker — began to develop the symptoms of the cancer that was to lead to his death. He consulted his doctor about the pain in October, 1948. Specialists were called in. Far from dispelling anxiety, they took a much more serious view of his illness than had been anticipated. King George gave orders that the bad news should be kept from Elizabeth until after her child was born. His Queen respected those wishes and not once did she betray her anxiety and the now heavy burden she was carrying.

Princess Elizabeth had hoped that the child would arrive on her first wedding anniversary, but in fact it was six days earlier, on November 14th, 1948, that a policeman announced to the waiting crowd: "It's a boy!" This time there was no embarrassed Home Secretary waiting to confirm this Royal birth. George VI had decided to kill off this tradition.

A NEW SOVEREIGN

LTHOUGH THERE had been happiness with the marriage of a daughter and future Queen to the man she loved, just as she, years before, had loved "Bertie", and the arrival of grand-children, the last few years of Elizabeth's life with her husband were clouded by his ill-health. He had to have an operation, lumbar sumpathectomy, to relieve thrombosis in his leg. Then, in 1951, came cancer. Throughout their life together the Queen Mother had taken some hard knocks, but this was the cruellest blow of all. For three years she knew her husband, who by this time she loved so dearly, was slowly dying.

She kept a smile in public, as did all the family, and those in the know gave the impression that nothing was wrong. George VI was alive . . . long live the King. How many women could keep so public a family together, give great comfort to a doomed husband, and still keep smiling? Extraordinary behaviour that is required of our Monarchy.

After the removal of his left lung, George VI never recovered his strength. But Elizabeth was there, as always, to give him her love, her confidence, her strength . . . though these, in the end, were not enough.

Everyone in the family and close advisers at Court realised how seriously ill George VI had become. He spent his last years enjoying the company of his grandchildren, who would stay with him and the Queen in Buckingham Palace and at Sandringham, while Elizabeth was visiting Philip in Malta. On one occasion when his elder daughter was away with Philip, he wrote: "Charles is too sweet, stumping around the room. We shall love having him at Sandringham. He is the fifth generation to live there and I hope he will get to like the place."

The King spent most of 1950 resting and trying to fight the malignant cancer that was destroying his lungs. He had to cancel public engagements and, where possible, Princess Elizabeth was carrying out duties on his behalf.

But by 1951 he was clearly a very sick man and in June his doctors diagnosed a "catarrhal inflammation of the right lung."

In between proudly showing their first-born to curious relatives, Elizabeth and Philip began giving some thought to naming the child. After the death of Albert, Prince Consort, Queen Victoria ruled that all male descendants should be named after her beloved husband. But they ignored orders from a previous century's Throne and decided to call him Charles Philip Arthur George.

The christening of the Queen Mother's first grandchild took place in the blue-columned Music Room overlooking the gardens at Buckingham Palace, for the Chapel had been bombed during the war. The gold lily font, made for the christening of the Princess Royal one hundred and eight years earlier and used to baptise the Royal mum when she was born, was brought from Windsor and filled with water from the River Jordan. Among the family circle at the service were four surviving grand-daughters of Queen Victoria, who had themselves worn the same lace christening robe. The ceremony was performed by the Archbishop of Canterbury, Dr. Fisher.

A few months after Charles arrived on the scene, the Royal Couple's first home of their own was ready. They moved into Clarence House, where the baby was settled down in a pale blue nursery. Within months Elizabeth

Continued on Page 145

A very early photograph of Elizabeth Angela Marguerite Bowes-Lyon, born 4th August, 1900, the ninth child of Lady Glamis.

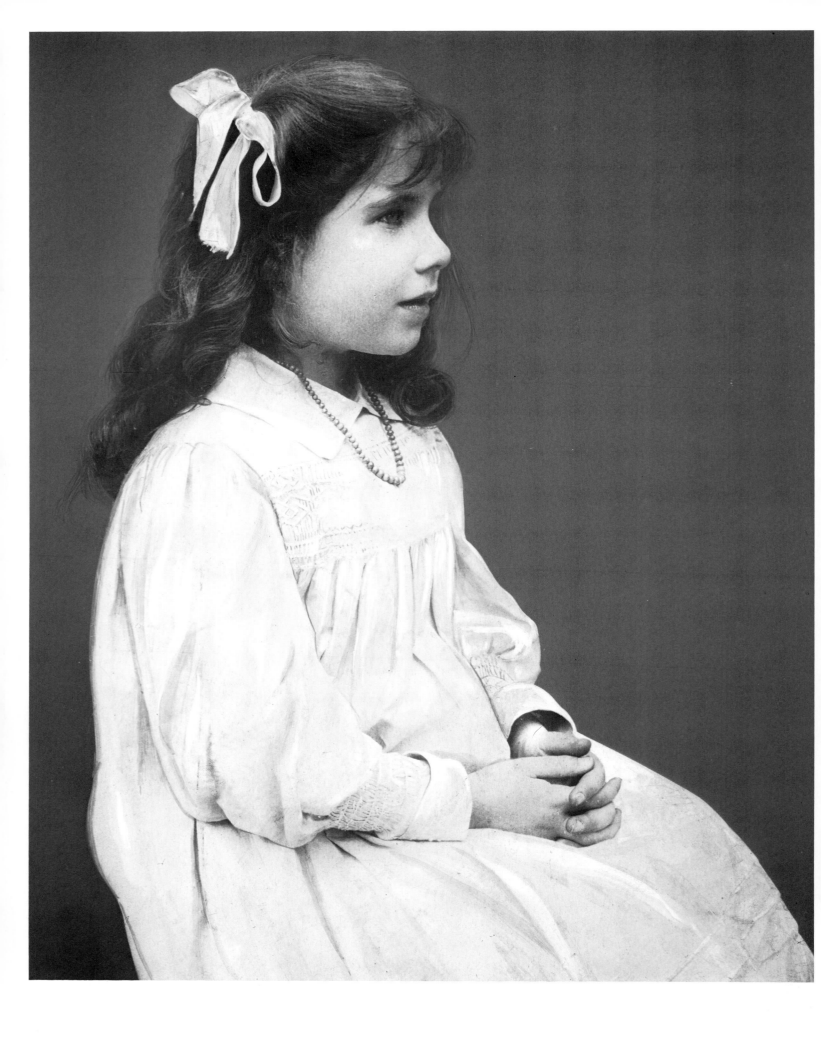

Portraits of the young Lady Elizabeth Bowes-Lyon (above) aged nine and on her pony, "Bobs" (right above) at St Paul's Waldenbury, near Welwyn, Hertfordshire. (Right) Elizabeth, again, still nine years of age, after a dancing lesson at Glamis Castle and (extreme right) as a seven-year-old: no smile for the camera this time!

(Left) Lady Elizabeth aged nine, poses for the camera at Glamis Castle and (above) with her brother, David.

Lady Elizabeth Bowes-Lyon with her father, the Earl of Strathmore (on the right) and her elder brother, Lord Glamis. This picture was taken just before Elizabeth's marriage to the Duke of York on 26th April, 1923.

The Duke and Duchess with Queen Mary during a holiday at Balmoral.

The Lady Elizabeth Bowes-Lyon pictured here as she leav

...er home on the way to her wedding to the Duke of York.

(Above) The Royal couple pose for official photographs inside Buckingham Palace. (Top right) The Duke and Duchess with their eight bridesmaids. (Bottom right) After the wedding, from left to right; The Prince of Wales (later Edward VIII), Princess Mary (the late Princess Royal), Prince Henry (late father of the present Duke of Gloucester), King George V, The Duke of York (later King George VI), Queen Mary and Prince George (late father of the present Duke of Kent).

43

(Left) Lady Elizabeth Bowes-Lyon, resplendent in her wedding dress. (Above) A Royal send-off for the newlyweds as they leave Buckingham Palace at the start of their honeymoon.

The Duke and Duchess of York at Polesden Lacy, in Surrey, where they spent the first part of their honeymoon in the May of 1923 (and right page).

An historic picture taken at Balmoral in September 1923, five months after the wedding. This picture shows t

oungest son of King George V and Queen Mary; Prince George, Queen Mary and the Duke and Duchess of York.

The new Duchess of York, thrust into the glare of public life after her marriage, became a trendsetter, as these pictures show. The long string of pearls, the dropped waist and (right) the Grecian look, all became very popular in the middle and late 1920s.

(Above) Stunning hats for a stunning lady. The Duchess sporting her favourite cloche hats which became all the rage in the early years of her marriage. (Right) Posing for posterity in a small tiara and pearls. The off the shoulder dress indicates that this picture was taken in the so-called 'Roaring Twenties' when bare arms and wide-cut necks were fashionable.

53

(Above and left) The Duke and Duchess of York are seen fulfilling their social obligations. The young couple were called upon to represent the Royal Family on many occasions. In addition there were private parties and days out to attend. (Opposite top) The Duke and Duchess of York arriving at Hendon Air Pageant on 30th June 1923 and (bottom) experiencing the thrill of an aerial railway at the Wembley Exhibition on another June day two years later.

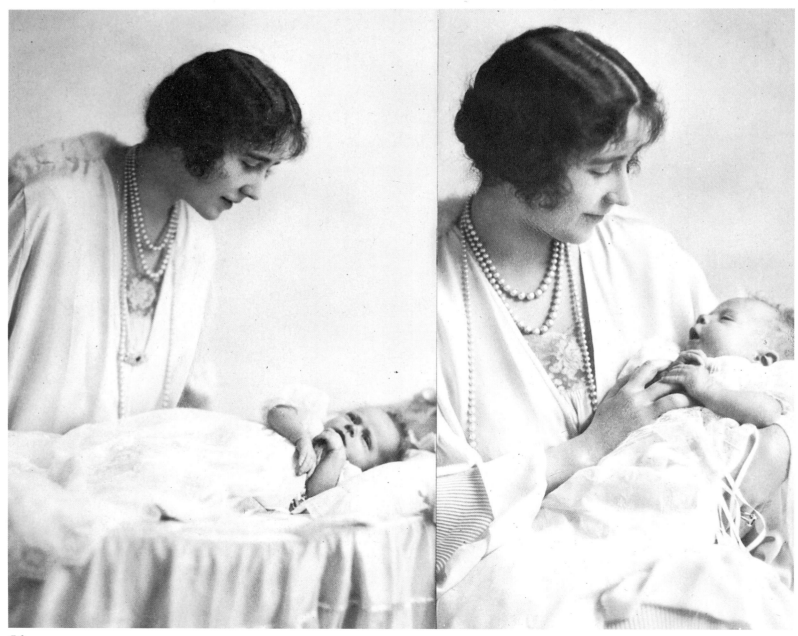

Left, the very first picture of Princess Elizabeth of York taken only a few weeks after her birth, being lovingly cared for by her mother, the Duchess of York.

(Above), The christening of Princess Elizabeth Alexandra Mary in 1926. Front (left to right), Lady Elphinstone, Her Majesty the Queen, the Duchess of York and baby Elizabeth, the Countess of Strathmore, Princess Mary and Viscountess Lascelles. Back row, the Duke of Connaught, His Majesty The King, the Duke of York and the Earl of Strathmore. (Right), The Duke and Duchess of York with baby Elizabeth.

(Above) Early photographs of the baby Princess with her mother. These pictures highlight the Duchess of York's exquisite beauty which became more apparent after the birth of her first child. (Top right) A family portrait of the Duke and Duchess with their daughter, aged 18 months. (Bottom right) The Duchess with Princess Elizabeth, then aged two.

(Above) The happy homecoming. The Duke and Duchess of York waving to crowds gathering outside their Piccadilly home to welcome them back to Britain after their Empire Tour in 1927. (Right) A close-up of the Royal Couple seen here on the balcony of Buckingham Palace on the same day. It was a joyous re-union for the Duchess and her one-year-old daughter.

The young Princess Elizabeth, aged three, has a tea-party for her parents in front of the cameras in July 192

The Duke, who hated to miss the fun and games, often accompanied his children on these photo-sessions.

The Duchess of York with Princess Elizabeth, aged two. These two studies highlight the close and happy relationship mother and daughter share to this day.

Copyright reserved–reproduced by gracious permission of Her Majesty The Queen.

Princess Elizabeth did not always want to pose for the cameras. Photographic sessions sometimes involved the Duchess trying to cajole her daughter into a smile, without much success in this particular case. These were taken in February 1931.

(Top) The Duchess of York with her second daughter Princess Margaret Rose a few weeks after the birth. (Bottom) Mother and daughter in profile. Margaret didn't take to the cameras quite so readily as her elder sister. (Right) Happy family portraits in 1931 when the children were five years and ten months respectively.

At Balmoral Castle for the holidays in 1933. The two young Princesses, Elizabeth and Margar

70

th their uncle, Heir to the Throne, Prince David, and their father, Prince Albert.

(Above) The Duke and Duchess of York with their daughters, who seem anxious not to miss anything, at St Paul's Cathedral in May 1935 for the Silver Jubilee of King George V and Queen Mary. (Right) Five months later in September 1935, The Duchess with Princesses Elizabeth and Margaret Rose.

The Duchess of York, always elegantly dressed, is captured for posterity escorting young Princesses Elizabeth and (above) Margaret Rose. Later as Queen (right), mother and daughters are even more in the public eye. The former Duchess knew where her duty lay, but for the young Princesses, it wasn't always so easy.

(Above) The Duchess of York with Princesses Elizabeth and Margaret in 1934. (Right) Family portraits of the Duke and Duchess and their children. The Duchess was especially photogenic, as these pictures show.

Copyright reserved (above). Reproduced by gracious permission of Her Majesty The Queen.

A day out for the Royals. The King and Queen with Princess Elizabeth.

Mother and daughter, Queen Elizabeth and Princess Elizabeth, sporting posies of flowers, show how much they enjoyed this Royal outing.

Both Princesses learned to play the piano. Here they are performing a duet for their mother in one of the upstairs parlours of Buckingham Palace.

Posing for the cameras can become tiresome, even when you're a Princess, as the expressions on Elizabeth and Margaret's faces show. Their mother is by now used to the constant attention of press and public. These pictures were taken during a Christmas holiday.

The summer provided a happy holiday for the Queen and the Princesses Elizabeth and Margaret Rose. A succession of happy, warm, summer days were spent at The Royal Lodge, Windsor. Here they are in the gardens at The Lodge.

(Above and right) The years spent at Royal Lodge were among the happiest of their lives for the Royal Children. The whole family loved dogs as these charming pictures show. Very often they seemed to be surrounded by an army of them.

Princess Elizabeth and Princess Margaret could play "houses" in their little Welsh cottage in the grounds of Royal Lodge, inviting Mummy and Daddy for tea-parties served at a knee high table. The cottage also provided plenty of room for their numerous dogs.

"Y Bwthyn Bach" is a miniature cottage presented to Princess Elizabeth and her sister by the people of Wales in 1931. The little house with the straw roof is child-sized, as can be seen from these pictures of the Duke and Duchess (above) with their daughters in the summer of 1936.

Daily Mirror

No. 10306   Registered at the G.P.O. as a newspaper.   ONE PENNY

EDWARD VIII WILL BROADCAST TO-NIGHT AS PRIVATE CITIZEN

Britain's new King and Queen, the Duke and Duchess of York. Their elder daughter, Princess Elizabeth, now ten years old, is heir to the Throne.

Picture pages are 8, 12 14, 16, 17, 19 and 28.

Edward VIII will broadcast to the Empire and the world to-night as a "private individual owing allegiance to the new King."

This will follow the signing of his abdication papers and the succession to the Throne of his brother, the Duke of York, who will be 41 on Monday.

The time has been fixed tentatively for 10 p.m.

EDWARD VIII's DESIRE TO SPEAK TO HIS PEOPLES DID NOT REACH THE B.B.C. UNTIL LATE LAST NIGHT. AT ONCE ARRANGEMENTS WERE MADE FOR THE MOST DRAMATIC BROADCAST THAT THE CORPORATION HAS EVER BEEN CALLED UPON TO HANDLE TO BE RELAYED TO ALL PARTS OF THE WORLD.

He may broadcast from Fort Belvedere, when it would be his last act on British soil before he goes abroad. Should he leave the country earlier in the evening, arrangements will be made for him to speak from abroad.

When his voice is heard to-night Edward VIII may, according to one belief, have become plain Mr. Edward Windsor.

Britain's new King, the Duke of York, some believe, may take the title of King George VI instead of Albert I. His wife will become Queen at thirty-six.

The two brothers dined together at Fort Belvedere last night and at a late hour were still occupied with State papers and official documents.

On returning to his home just before midnight the Duke's car was mobbed and took some minutes to drive the last few yards into the forecourt of the house.

The great multitude stood outside and sang the National Anthem. "For He's a Jolly Good Fellow," and chanted in unison "We want our King and Queen."

EMPIRE HEARS NEWS
WITH UTMOST CALM

The dramatic announcement of abdication made in the House of Commons yesterday was received with the utmost calm throughout the Empire.

In London the vast crowds which gathered in Whitehall, Downing-street and Piccadilly, last night, were comparatively quiet save for demonstrations by a few hooligans.

They sang "God Save the King!" they sang "For He's a Jolly Good Fellow!" they shouted "We Want King Albert!"

A man with a megaphone marched at the head of a party which came along the Mall, shouting "Long Live King Albert!"

Crowds gathered near Downing-street, too, last night. At ten o'clock the little street was cleared and a cordon of police guarded the Whitehall entrance.

Three minutes later several hundred Fascists came running down Whitehall from Trafalgar-square, shouting at the top of their voices and brandishing newspapers.

(Continued on back page)

(Above) Friday 11th December 1936 changed the lives of the Duke and Duchess of York for ever. His brother, Edward VIII, abdicated and 'Bertie' became King, and Elizabeth, Queen. (Top right) King George VI and Queen Elizabeth passing Admiralty Arch on their way to Westminster Abbey for his Coronation on 12th May, 1937. (Bottom right) After camping out all night the thousands of sightseers were determined not to miss a thing—so cardboard periscopes were the order of the day.

Impressive scenes inside Westminster Abbey during the Coronation ceremony of King George VI.

(Above) The Archbishop of Canterbury, having taken the Queen's Crown from the Altar, placed it upon her head and pronounced: "Receive the Crown of Glory, Honour and Joy . . ." (Right) The newly crowned King and Queen, with Queen Mary and the Princesses Elizabeth and Margaret, greet the crowds outside Buckingham Palace after the Coronation.

Balcony scenes following the Coronation. King George VI and Queen Elizabeth with Queen Mary and Princesses Elizabeth and Margaret, together with ladies-in-waiting and pages, on the balcony at Buckingham Palace acknowledging the jubilant cheers of the crowds below.

A solemn moment for the Royal Family after the coronation of George VI. Princess Elizabeth was eleven and Princess Margaret Rose six. (Left) The whole family, dressed in Coronation robes, trains and crowns, pose in the Throne Room at Buckingham Palace. (Above) The new King and Queen.

An official picture of King George VI and Queen Elizabeth in 1937.

The King and Queen dressed for a State function. The King is wearing his Ceremonial Dress uniform.

The war is looming. This charming picture of King George VI and Queen Elizabeth with their children was taken at Buckingham Palace in 1939. (Right) The following year the family pose again for the camera, this time at Windsor on the eve of Princess Elizabeth's fourteenth birthday.

A picture of the Royal Family to warm the hearts

...tain and the Commonwealth during the war years.

Enjoyable family afternoons recorded at the Royal Lodge, Windsor during the war years. (Above) A knitting session for the two young Princesses. (Below) A seat in the shade for Mother and daughters—and the favourite family dog. —— (Right) An informal picture of the Queen and the two Princesses, here aged fourteen and ten, taken in 1940.

(Above) April 1940 and Princess Elizabeth, who was approaching her fourteenth birthday, is seen in the grounds of the Royal Lodge at Windsor with her mother. (Top right) Queen Elizabeth with her daughters in 1942 and (bottom right) the Royal Family in the grounds of the Royal Lodge at Windsor just before Princess Elizabeth's sixteenth birthday.

Princesses Elizabeth and Margaret in the grounds of Windsor Castle with the Queen in 1941. The Royal children spent most of the war years at Windsor where they did their studying. The Queen travelled to Buckingham Palace each day, but returned with the King to the relative safety of Windsor Castle at night.

This study of mother and daughters was tak

Windsor Castle in the summer of 1941.

King and Queen examine the damage caused by a German bomber to the quadrangle of Buckingham Palace. The Palace

at the Pa

cked twice during raids in September 1940. The King and his family, who slept at Windsor during the raids, were always back
aylight.

THE WAR YEARS

A new and terrifying chapter in her life lay ahead for the Queen Mother. Like millions of others she was caught up in the horrifying conflict of World War Two. Throughout it, she was a guide and an inspiration not only to her husband but to the nation. (Left) Prime Minister Winston Churchill with the King and Queen after visiting Buckingham Palace to inspect the bomb damage. Often the King and Queen went into the streets of London to cheer up people who had lost their homes in the blitz. (above) The Royal Couple in the East End after one such raid.

King George and Que

izabeth visiting A.R.P. units.

Lost in the crowd! King George VI and Queen Elizabeth (above and right) accompanied by the Lord and Lady Mayoress of Sheffield visiting bombed areas of the city in 1941. The Royal Couple always found time to talk to those made homeless.

(Top) A walk with the workers at a Ministry of Supply Ordnance Factory. (Bottom) The King and Queen taking the salute as Scottish troops move off on manoeuvres.

(Top) King and Queen with Princess Elizabeth in a Scout car during their inspection of the Royal Artillery. (Bottom) Their Majesties peer into the engine of an Army car, watched by Princess Elizabeth (in ATS uniform) and Princess Margaret Rose.

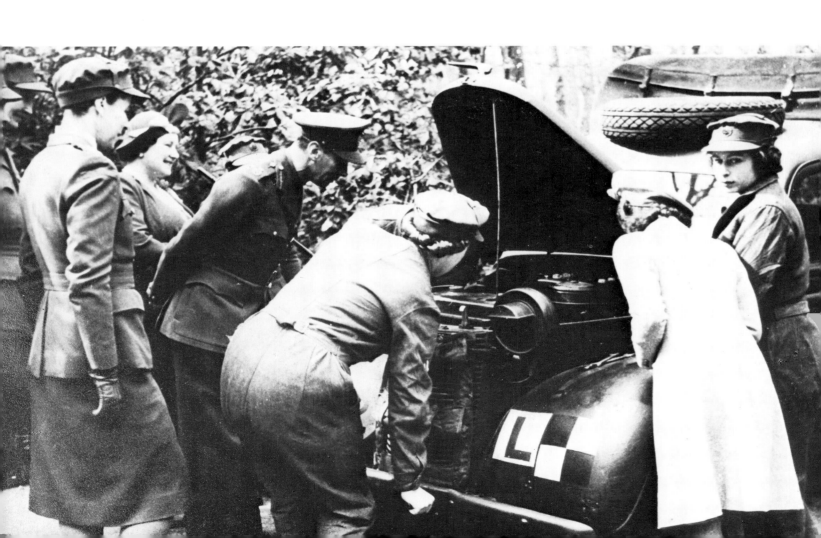

The Royal Family at home in 1942. This intimate fireside parlour scene shows the young Elizabeth knitting
for the Forces while her mother and sister's attention is taken by something the King is reading.
(Right) Informal studies inside Buckingham Palace—the Queen serves her husband
afternoon tea and later enjoys a game of patience while King George
reads the newspaper.

Harvest time during the war years on the Sandringham estate. T

yal Family take a trip around the fields to see the work of the combines.

125

The park at Sandringham House became a farm during the war years. Here the K

Queen with their daughters inspect a partially harvested crop of barley in 1943.

ROYAL WAR EFFORT. The King and Queen toured the country lifting the spirits of those on the Home Front. He

 Queen is chatting to women workers in a Berkshire field in 1944. The end of the war was still a year away.

(Left) The King and his family arrive for an evening out at a G.I.'s show. (Above) The Royal Family stand to attention on the dais at the stand-down ceremony of the Windsor Home Guard.

131

V.E. Day. From left: Princess Elizabeth; Queen Elizabeth; the Prime Minister, Sir Winston Churchill; King Georg

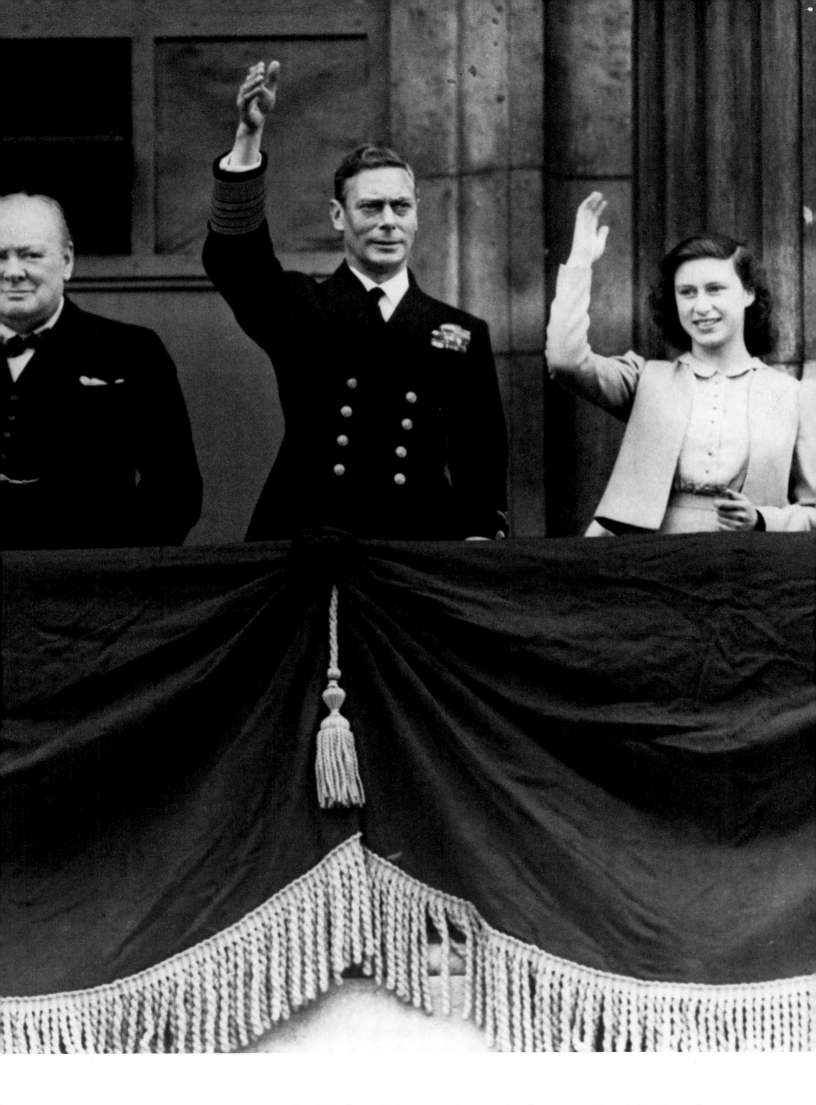

and Princess Margaret on the balcony of Buckingham Palace waving to the huge crowd celebrating victory.

Top) King George VI and Queen Elizabeth joined by Queen Mary and other dignitaries on the Royal Dais in the Mall to view the Victory Parade on V.E. Day 8th June 1945. (Above) Princesses Elizabeth and Margaret watching and waiting for the parade to pass.

(Top) King George VI salutes as the parade passes and (above) a moment to relax for the Royal Family on the dais as they watch more soldiers approaching. Note the leading politicians of the day.

A Sunday afternoon in the summer of 1946 and the Princesses Elizabeth and Margaret relax with their parents in the gardens of the Royal Lodge at Windsor.

Still at Royal Lodge, and enjoying the sunshine as this charming, peaceful scene show

he war is a year behind them and now the King and Queen face new challenges.

King George VI and Queen Elizabeth with Princesses Elizabeth and Margaret at Buckingham Palace in 1946. The portra particular, has the air of

stiffly formal and carefully posed, despite the photographer's efforts to create an informal atmosphere: King George in
an sitting for a portrait.

An informal picture (above) of Princess Elizabeth laughing with her father at Royal Lodge in the summer of 1946. (Right) The whole family pose, with the dog, in the beautiful gardens (and overleaf).

142

was pregnant again. Princess Anne Elizabeth Alice Louise was also born there, a few days after Philip had dashed back from Naval duties to be with his wife. The only grand-daughter in the family was christened, like her elder brother, in the Palace Music Room. In September, after the King's chest had been X-rayed and specimens of lung tissue taken, the King had an operation to remove his left lung. He appeared to recover, though he was much thinner, looked even older, and had difficulty with his voice.

In October it was announced that, owing to the King's illness, he and the Queen would not be able to go on their planned tour of East Africa, Australia and New Zealand in 1952 and that Princess Elizabeth and Philip would go in their place.

By November the King was well enough to be photographed with Prince Charles on his third birthday, and early in December he introduced Princess Elizabeth and the Duke of Edinburgh as members of the Privy Council, his closest group of advisers. By this time Philip had returned from Naval service in Malta to help his wife with her increasing burden of Royal duties. He and the Princess carried out their first tour of North America, missing Charles's birthday in November.

During the tour of Canada and the United States, Elizabeth carried with her a sealed envelope to be opened in the event of her father's death. It contained her Accession Documents, giving her immediate powers of Sovereignty.

A bad cough forced George to undergo a second bronchoscopy just before Christmas, when his annual broadcast to Britain and the Commonwealth revealed the struggle he was having with his voice. He underwent another examination on January 29th, 1952, and his doctors said they were pleased with his progress.

The next evening, the entire family went to see the musical, *South Pacific,* at Drury Lane Theatre as a celebration of the King's recovery, and as a farewell to Princess Elizabeth and the Duke of Edinburgh before they left the next day for their five-month tour of East Africa, Australia and New Zealand.

The following morning, 56-year-old George VI stood hatless on the tarmac of Heathrow Airport to bid farewell to his daughter and son-in-law. His gaunt appearance as he and Elizabeth waved goodbye shook those watching. He appeared like a man who truly knew he was facing death as he gave a last wave to his Lilibet.

The sixth of February, 1952, was a day when Prince Philip and Elizabeth were resting in the Aberdare Game Reserve in Kenya after an exhausting first few days of their East African tour. The Royal Party were staying in a hut built in the branches of a giant fig tree. It overlooked a watering hole where animals came in the middle of the night. Elizabeth had stayed up until dawn watching elephant, rhinoceros and water-buck through binoculars.

BY 10.45 a.m. LONDON TIME — 1.45 p.m. in Kenya — it had been announced that King George VI had died in his sleep at Sandringham during the night. He was discovered by his assistant valet, James Macdonald, when he went into the King's room at 7.30 a.m. Princess Elizabeth had been Queen for several hours — but how long will never be known. The exact timing of her Accession cannot be fixed because no one was with George when he died. History will have to be satisfied that she knew she had become Sovereign at 2.45 in the afternoon, Kenyan time — 11.45 in the morning 4,000 miles away in Britain. She was twenty-five.

Back in London, when, early in the morning, the Prime Minister, Winston Churchill was told of the King's death, he sat in bed, gazing at the walls of his room, tears in his eyes and scarcely able to speak. "I really did love him," he said. "His advice was so good and I could always count on his support in times of difficulty. I hardly know Princess Elizabeth, and she is only a child."

Her Majesty Queen Elizabeth II of Great Britain and her Dominions, together with her Consort, Philip, and entourage, flew through the night, via Libya, to begin her reign. She arrived back at Heathrow Airport at four o'clock on the afternoon of Thursday, February 7th. Dressed in black, she walked alone down the steps of the aircraft to where Churchill and her other Ministers stood waiting with their heads bowed. "This is a very tragic homecoming," she told them.

From the airport she drove to the centre of her capital city and down the Mall for the first time as Queen to Clarence House. At 4.30 a limousine drove slowly out of the gates to nearby Marlborough House. Inside was Queen Mary. "Her old Grannie and subject must be the first to kiss Her hand," she said. As she curtseyed to her grand-daughter, the new Queen's Royal Standard was raised on the roof of Clarence House.

That night Churchill broadcast an oration which was to be compared with his finest wartime speeches. Mainly in tribute to the dead King, but he recalled that Elizabeth was the name of England's greatest Queen. He ended: "I, whose youth was passed in the august, unchallenged and tranquil glories of the Victorian era, may well feel a thrill in invoking once more the prayer and the anthem, 'God Save the Queen'."

Queen Elizabeth II was proclaimed at 11.00 o'clock on the morning of 8th February, 1952, on the balcony of St. James's Palace, next door to Clarence House. St. James's is the official State Palace. For example, new ambassadors are accredited to the Court of St. James'!

In the Throne Room at St. James's Palace, the young Queen held her first Privy Council. Then she joined her mother and other members of the family at Sandringham and walked behind the dead King's coffin as it was borne to the Church of St. Mary Magdalene, across the park from the house. On 11th February the King's body was taken by train to London for Lying-in-State in Westminster Hall, where more than 300,000 people queued, in bitterly cold weather, to file past the coffin.

Among the callers at Clarence House was the widowed Queen. The Queen Mother had to bow to the new Sovereign. She was desolate, but she kept her feelings hidden. Protocol demanded that she sent a message to the millions around the world who shared her sadness:

> "Your concern for me has upheld me in my sorrow and how proud you have made me by your wonderful tributes to

my dear husband, a great and noble King. No man had a deeper sense than he of duty and of service, and no man was more full of compassion for his fellow men.

"He loved you all, every one of you, most truly. That, you know, was what he always tried to tell you in his yearly message at Christmas; that was the pledge he took at the sacred moment of his Coronation fifteen years ago.

"Now I am left alone, to do what I can to honour that pledge without him. Throughout our married life, we have tried, the King and I, to fulfil with all our hearts and all our strength the great task of service that was laid upon us. My only wish now is that I may be allowed to continue the work we sought to do together.

"I commend to you our dear daughter: give her your loyalty and devotion; in the great and lonely station to which she has been called she will need your protection and love.

"God bless you all; and may He in His wisdom guide us safely to our true destiny of peace and goodwill. *Elizabeth R.*"

After the statement had been published it was noticed that an omission had been made. There was no mention of Queen Elizabeth II's Consort or the two children. Hastily, officials set the record straight by phoning newspaper editors to tell them that the reference to the new Queen should have read: *"I commend to you our dear daughter; give her your loyalty and devotion. Though blessed in her husband and children, she will need your protection and your love in the great and lonely station to which she has been called."*

The King was buried in St. George's Chapel, Windsor. On the coffin rested a wreath of white orchids, white lilies and white carnations from the Queen Mother. A card read: *"For darling Bertie, from his always loving Elizabeth."*

There had been a moment of anguish before the funeral. Prince Charles asked her when Grandpa was coming back to play soldiers with him. The widow hugged her grandson to her and could not answer. The three-year-old Prince noticed that his nurses were in tears and said softly: "Don't cry, Granny."

The Queen Mother was soon out and about again, doing the rounds of garden parties, military reviews, ceremonials and the rest. But she went to great lengths not to overshadow her daughter. In whatever she did, the Queen Mother made it clear that she was now Number Two . . . Britain had a new Elizabethan Age.

The 51-year-old ex-Queen refused to allow sorrow to overcome her, though. Within a day of her husband's death she was playing with her grandchildren, Charles and Anne. "I have got to start sometime and it is better now than later," she told one of her aides.

SHE DECIDED to find a new role for herself, not wishing to emulate Queen Victoria as a widow constantly in black.

So it was that in 1952, Her Majesty began a "third life" — as Queen Mother. She has been the Royal Dowager for more than forty years, twice as long as she was Queen Consort. To millions she is the ideal of acceptable Royalty.

Now that her daughter reigned, Elizabeth was the Second Lady in the land. She still had the status of a Queen and was still referred to as Her Majesty. Every woman in the land, except the Sovereign, was expected to curtsey to her, and every man to bow. Even Philip kissed his mother-in-law's hand, and Charles and Anne were taught to bow and curtsey before rushing into their grand mother's arms.

The title of Queen Mother was adopted to distinguish her from the new Sovereign.

It is not one favoured in Royal circles — Elizabeth's staff still refer to her as Queen Elizabeth. But she was obliged to adopt it because of possible confusion with her daughter, and since she did her popularity has actually increased. The love and respect shown to Elizabeth has never been so marked as now when to millions of people throughout the world she became "The Queen Mum."

In the various Royal households Elizabeth II is referred to simply as The Queen, and her mother as Queen Elizabeth.

Society photographer and friend Cecil Beaton observed: "I did not realise how life can be ruthless, even to Queens. We all know what happened to Henry's six wives, and certainly today we have become a bit more civilised; but still human nature can be pretty base. Through a sad break of fortune Queen Elizabeth loses her husband at an early age, and from that very moment her position in life is changed completely. Although she is undoubtedly treated with great love, consideration and sympathy by her daughter who is now reigning Monarch . . . nevertheless, no doubt unknown to the present Queen, her mother is suddenly given quite casual treatment by many at Buckingham Palace."

The costs of her public duties and keeping her forty-strong staff are met by her allowance under the Civil List, raised by 3¼ per cent in the 1985 Budget to £345,300 per annum.

When she's out and about on her travels she tries to make sure that expenditure on her behalf is kept to a minimum. For example, she worries about going too often to the Cinque Ports in case the cost of entertaining proves heavy on the rates. She frequently advises town clerks to cut down their suggested six-course luncheons in favour of light buffets.

Central London is a "Royal Village" running East from Kensington High Street, to Hyde Park Corner, South to Buckingham Palace, and East again to Clarence House, St. James's Palace and York House.

Princess Margaret, the Countess of Athlone and the Duke and Duchess of Gloucester live at the Kensington Palace end. The Duke and Duchess of Kent live at York House, butting on to St. James's Palace, and Clarence House is the official home of the Queen Mother.

It is attached to St. James's Palace, but is a separate household. Elizabeth has made it a home of taste and elegance. This is despite it's many drawbacks. It is really three houses, the front house standing back to back with two smaller houses in Ambassador's Court, abuts on to St. James's Palace, with which it has a connecting door. This makes it a house with awkwardly-sited doors connecting its two halves, and many passages, difficult to work and to live in.

But the Queen Mother enjoys living there. She usually rises early and reads most of the papers except "the pops" breakfasting in her room with *The Sporting Life*, *The Times*, *Telegraph*, *Mail* and *Express*, and easing into the day's work at 11.00, when her private secretary knocks on her door for their morning conference.

She never rests in the afternoon, and after years of Royal practice actually prefers standing up to sitting down. She can still stand for hours at a time — to the dismay of courtiers much younger, who, of course, have to do the same.

When spending a rare evening alone at home, she will watch television or write letters for a few hours before retiring at about 11.00.

She watches television, with a penchant for old comedies. "*Dad's Army*" was her favourite. Recently "*Yes, Minister*" has proved an acceptable substitute.

By the time the Queen Mother reached her 50th birthday she had proved herself the most successful Queen Consort in history. She had sustained a King and inspired a country through Abdication and wartime blitz. She had always been regal, but at the same time *real*, blessed with the ability to draw others to her.

The Times said of her character thus: "She speaks to all men and women on the level of common experience . . . She is never afraid to challenge the over-sophisticated . . . she ignores the cynics and the pessimists and holds up for admiration the things that are lovely and of good report."

She has clocked up an amazing record. She had become the oldest person to bear the title of Queen in the history of the British Monarchy, surpassing the previous record-holder, her mother-in-law, Queen Mary. And she is still going strong. Her taxing round of Royal engagements make her one of the hardest-working pensioners in the country.

There were no special celebrations to mark the record when she reached her 86th birthday. "She's far too busy," her Clarence House staff said. "It is very much business as usual" a spokesman added. "She has a full summer programme ahead of her meeting people all round the country."

The next day she went off to Gateshead, Tyne and Wear, to inspect an industrial estate and visit a hospital. The following day she was back in London for a night out at the ballet. Then there was a garden party in Chelsea.

She actually enjoys having her diary full of engagements and organisations planning great occasions wonder: "Can we get *Her* to come?" If she does accept an invitation it is certain that at some moment she will slip through the line-up of directors and managers and have a word with the office boys and the typists stuck in the back row.

These days she has started to take life a little more slowly. But she can still fulfil a day of engagements and she seems to become livelier as the day moves on. Yet she has always maintained she is basically lazy. At one time she kept a notice on her desk which read "DO IT NOW" — though she never believed it had the slightest effect.

The Queen Mother is not one of the dashers-about of this world. She is not renowned for her speed in clearing a desk of papers, nor does she always arrive for appointments on time. But such is her genuine interest in people she invariably runs behind schedule.

She is always a little behind time, talking to one of the officials or his wife while the equerry and lady-in-waiting look at their watches. It is often a frustrating job for photographers at a Royal occasion. Officials, police and detectives sometimes make their task difficult. Even so, the Queen Mother is their favourite Royal. When she spots them she halts and smiles, and if she knows one of them of old has a few words and asks about his family while the officials try hard to smile.

"I need them," she said once, "just as much as they need me."

She has always been the favourite among Press photographers because she invariably takes the trouble to pause well within lens range and turn in their direction. In a presentation line-up she usually pauses to talk to someone about four persons from the end — a handy distance for the cameramen.

Coupled with all this activity is a full, private life which, if not spent with either her grandchildren or great-grandchildren, is kept fully occupied by her keen interest in horse racing.

Once, on hearing that a chiropodist friend was ill, she called on his home to offer wishes for a speedy recovery. And, on another occasion in Scotland, she drove 160 miles out of her way to sip tea with a retired maid who had served her for thirty years.

Among the strange associations she has is membership of one of Britain's tightest union closed shops. The Transport and General Workers Union made her an honorary member of their Smithfield meat porters' branch. It happened after she visited the London market and was enrolled as a porter — with the right to drink in Smithfield's open-all-hours pubs. She was also given an arm-band indicating that she was a "bummaree" — the slang term for a porter.

Later she accepted union leader Ron Todd's written offer of a union card — which pointed out that her husband, King George VI, had also become a member after a Smithfield visit. As her membership is honorary, she doesn't have to decide whether or not to pay the union political levy to the Labour Party.

OVER THE YEARS there have been losses of relatives and friends. The most distressing was the death in 1961 of her brother, Sir David Bowes-Lyon, who had remained close and dear to his sister throughout adult life. He had lived with his wife Rachel, at St. Paul's Walden Bury, the childhood home. He died, at fifty-nine, while on holiday at Birkhall. They buried him at the Hertfordshire home beside the lawns and enchanted woodlands where a small Elizabeth and David played together fifty years before.

Her brother-in-law, the Duke of Gloucester, next in age to her husband, died in 1974, two years after his elder son, Prince William, had been killed in an air race. But the greatest tragedy of all apart from the loss of her husband was the murder of Earl Mountbatten of Burma.

It was a terrible blow to the Queen Mother. She had known him for more than fifty years.

He had been a close friend of both her husband and the Duke of Windsor. She had admired his courage during the war as a Naval captain, as a brilliant commander-in-chief, and, after the war, as the last Viceroy of India before independence.

Lord Mountbatten was almost as popular with the public as herself, certainly in the later stages of his life. Like her, he was able to inspire, though his appeal sprang from being an extrovert, a natural and brilliant showman. He was one of the late King George's VI's closest friends and once paid this tribute to the Queen Mother: "The one thing I wanted him to have was a wife who would look after him, make him proud of himself. Remember, he was totally overshadowed by his elder brother, the Prince of Wales. He needed someone to bring him out, above all give him confidence, and that is precisely what she did. He was shy, he had this stammer, but she pushed him forward — and made him happy."

"When he died, she never did this Queen Victoria thing, parading around that frightful public grief, though the King's death absolutely shattered her, I know. He has never been out of her thoughts, but she was determined no one else would know it."

Although she is credited with having done much to "democratise" the Royal Family, to have taken the first steps, she had always felt that Lord Mountbatten deserved most of the credit.

It is now going on for seven years since the brutal murder of Lord Mountbatten, his 14-year-old grandson and a teenage friend by Irish terrorists. It happened when a bomb, planted on his fishing boat, was detonated by a radio signal as he sailed near his holiday home in the Irish Republic.

The Queen Mother was on holiday on Deeside with her family nearby. The Queen, who was at Balmoral, heard on the radio the news that invoked world-wide condemnation. Her Majesty immediately drove over to Birkhall to comfort her mother.

The Royal Family's "Uncle Dickie" was almost exactly the same age as Elizabeth. She showed little outward sign of shock and grief. It was left to the Prince of Wales to express the family's deep sense of loss at a memorial service in St. Paul's. He spoke, with rare public anger, of the "mindless cruelty" of the killers and of the "vulnerability of civilised democracy and freedom to the kind of subhuman extremism which blows people up when it feels like it."

But of course, life goes on and the Queen Mother continues furnishing Clarence House with fine antiques and paintings. She still studies auction catalogues carefully, and if she finds something she thinks might be interesting, one of her household visits the sale-room to bid. She is especially attracted by an antique or painting that has some connection with her own family, and she has a particular taste for Regency wine coasters.

When any of her racing friends come to lunch she may have one of her racing cups displayed on the table.

The Queen Mother enjoys light reading and likes to sit with a book in the drawing room when the sun is pouring through the windows. Or perhaps she will play something on the grand piano. Many happy hours have been spent by the Queen Mother and her children and grandchildren round the piano singing songs from hit musicals or Scottish ballads.

She also derives great pleasure from her fabulous collection of jewels. It is so dazzling that she is sometimes called "the Pearly Queen." She is rarely seen without either tiara or hat-off-the-face, flowered, feathered or veiled — and never without that distinctive three-string set of pearls, which she is said to wear even while out fishing in the Dee.

Few women have such jewellery as the Queen Mother. Their total value would be impossible to calculate because no part of the collection is ever likely to come on the open market. Most pieces have been passed down from one generation to the next, and the practice is likely to continue.

Her favourite pieces are those given to her by her family, particularly magnificent gems presented to her by her husband over the years. There is, for example, a Naval cap badge, depicted in diamonds, which he gave to her at the time of their engagement; a necklace of diamonds and pearls, with a pendant to match, which was his wedding present to her. Just after his Coronation he produced a jewelled Thistle Badge and Star,

which he had secretly prepared because there was only one in the Crown Jewels collection.

The Crown that she wore at her husband's Coronation was specially made, and displayed the famous Koh-i-Noor diamond which had been removed from Queen Mary's Crown. The four diamond-studded arches can be detached, leaving a circlet which the Queen Mother has worn on several occasions, including the ceremony of her daughter's Coronation.

The Queen Mother has access to certain of the Crown Jewels, but she also has a large collection of personal jewellery. One item which she wears frequently is a honeycomb tiara, with star tips standing above the main design. Originally, it was given to Queen Mary, and is set with magnificent South African diamonds.

Jewellery is important to the Queen Mother as a woman. She enjoys setting it off against the colours of the dress she is wearing, whether it be a ball gown or a short dress. She has some beautiful and priceless pearl necklaces, but also a large collection of lapel brooches, which she wears just because she likes them, or, quite often, because they have a special connection with the people or place she is going to visit.

SOMETIMES SHE can be sheer sparkle from tiara to toe. Gems adorn her gowns on every possible occasion whether in full-dress suits in town or in tweeds in the country. She has an unashamed love of glitter. She knows her jewellery, and extravagantly indulges her whims on some occasions.

She did that in a spectacular way a few years ago during one State Visit when she decided that she would like to wear the Koh-i-noor diamond, the thousand-year-old gem from India, at a State banquet. This magnificent stone was given to Queen Victoria in 1850 by the East India Company, and is one of the Crown Jewels kept guarded in the Tower of London.

Messages were dispatched, doors unlocked, the jewel was boxed and sent with an escort to the Queen Mother's home, where it was placed under guard.

In the end she did not wear it. She changed her mind.

For more than 40 years the Queen Mother's dress style was strictly along lines laid down by the couturier, the late Sir Norman Hartnell. The Queen Mother "look" is usually as follows . . .

The colour is often one of her favourites — turquoise. The basic design is a dress with cross-over top and a tied belt. Over that, in the same material and colour, is draped a coat-skirt cut on classical lines.

The sleeves are cut short on top of the wrist, falling away fully below. The gloves are worn as the Queen Mother invariably wears them, ruched.

She has a particular characteristic, incidentally, seen also in Princess Margaret. Her hands are very small and delicate with, even today, milky, smooth skin. It is a pity she always wears gloves in public because only her close friends and family are able to see those elegant hands.

At the shoulder she usually wears a brooch and three rows of pearls round the neck. The ensemble is topped off by an ostrich-feather trimmed hat. A handbag, often not matching either the style or colour of the outfit, completes the picture.

She refers to her clothes, especially the more grand affairs, as her "props." Norman Hartnell worshipped her. Until his death, in 1979, he sent her a bouquet of red roses on her birthday.

Her clothes today are still made by Hartnell's salon, but she no longer needs the number that she used to and she has favourite dresses and coats that come out again and again. She sometimes hangs on to a particular handbag for years. She still has an umbrella with a gold pencil fitted into the handle which she's had since her wedding.

She set a style for elegance in the Twenties, which she has always tried to maintain. When she opened a sale of work it was noted by a fashion writer of the era: "She looked such a sweet-faced, pretty, gentle-natured girl as she appreciatively handled the lovely work and thanked the organisers. She wore a *cafe-au-lait* brown duvetine skirt and loose Russian-shaped coat to match, a row of pearls around her lovely neck and a big black straw hat trimmed with soft black and gold ribbon."

After her marriage she discovered that Bertie had strong likes and dislikes about women's fashions. For instance, he did not like to see the Duchess of York in green. During the war it was said that another reason she did not wear this colour was because it was considered unlucky. Whatever the reason the Queen Mother was not seen in green until after her husband's death.

Away from the public eye she likes to spend her days quietly with a few close friends and her grandchildren. She is very informal in private. She once told a companion to turn down the sound on television when the National Anthem was being played. "When you're not present, it's like hearing the Lord's Prayer while playing canasta," she explained.

Depending on the time of year, she lives in the Royal Lodge at Windsor, Clarence House in London, where she does most of her entertaining, or at three homes in Scotland.

Summer usually finds her at Birkhall, a mansion on the River Dee, and not far from the rest of the family at Balmoral, or at either Glamis Castle or the Castle of Mey, a lonely gale-swept place in Caithness in the far North of Scotland, one of her greatest extravagances.

There have been stories of ghosts haunting Glamis Castle, her ancestral home where Princess Margaret was born. It is said to attract all manner of spirits. There's the Tongueless Woman who stands pale-faced at a barrel window, giving one of the castle turrets a most severe look; the old Earl of Beardie, cursing and stamping around the room that once was his; a weird fellow called Jack the Runner, who goes darting off here and there whenever the moon peeps through; and other ghosts, with lesser claims to fame!

When top ghost hunter Peter Underwood, a senior member of the Society of Psychical Research, called at Glamis he was told rather coolly: "Ghostly associations with the castle are not stressed any more."

When she acquired Mey Castle many thought it signalled the end of her public life: it was so far removed from any of the other Royal residences, and the purchase was made at a particularly sad time.

It was during the weeks following her husband's death, when reaction had set in and she was feeling desperately lonely and uncertain. She went to stay with old friends at their home on the Caithness coast. One afternoon, while they were out for a drive, they paid a visit to the ancient Barrogill Castle, which had been up for sale for some time without attracting a buyer. Her hosts told the Queen Mother it was likely that the castle would be demolished. "Never!" she protested. "I'll buy it." And so she did, and changed the name back to Mey, the name it had when an Earl of Caithness rebuilt it 400 years ago. "I felt a great wish to preserve, if I could, this ancient dwelling."

Perhaps the original reason, subconsciously, was to have somewhere to hide away in her desolation. Very soon the old building, with its neglected garden and surrounding acres of austere landscape stretching to a rugged coastline, revitalised her.

"It is a delight to me now that I have a home in Caithness," she told the citizens of Wick on receiving the freedom of their town. "A country of such great beauty, combining, as it does, the peace and tranquillity of an open and uncrowded countryside with the rugged glory of a magnificent coastline — the remote detachment of country villages with the busy and independent life of your market towns."

Today, she spends around ten weeks each summer at Mey, interspersed with some time just eight miles away from Balmoral at Birkhall.

When George VI died she inherited capital and private estates worth several million pounds, and it was these funds that she used to buy what was a grim, tumbledown dwelling with wind howling through the Macbeth-like chill corridors.

The Sixteenth-Century castle was an incredibly dilapidated old place, ripe for demolition, riddled with the damp and the black peat smoke of centuries.

The bleak building of pink stone was an abandoned dwelling near the shore of the stormy Pentland Firth. Barrogill Castle, until Her Majesty came along, had no prospect of ever being bought and restored.

But there was something about the place, and its setting so soon after the King's death, that appealed to the romantic Scot in her. Perhaps it was a sense of history, who knows. But soon one of her most absorbing pastimes was restoring the old walls and planning to furnish the interior to her own taste. It took several years before Mey was fully recreated, though.

Throughout, she kept in touch with every detail: the roofing, the laying on of water and electricity, the refitting of bathrooms, the installing of comfortable furniture, the hanging of pictures, the cleaning of outside walls and paths, and the taming of the overgrown garden.

Over the years she has installed central heating, and furnished the castle with pieces of furniture from auctions. One of her most recent acquisitions was a rug woven behind bars by an admiring prisoner who based the pattern on the colours of her coat-of-arms — gold, blue and green.

The Queen Mother favoured a decorative style of warm-coloured furnishings and white walls, leaving the stone-flagged floors of the hall and staircase partly covered with coconut matting. Her own sitting room is in one of the towers. It has a barrel-vaulted ceiling and thick walls, but is made cosy by chintz-covered easy chairs and a Stuart tartan fireside rug.

Adjoining the Castle she has a flock of sheep and a herd of Aberdeen Angus cattle. She markets the produce from the old garden whose fine fruit and vegetables are high-walled against the gales from the Arctic.

It is her personal haven. She loves the mellowed and very private castle, its sparse local population and its bleak farmlands.

The people of nearby Caithness love having the Queen Mother among them; hearing her talk about The Swirlies and The Twirlies — the names the locals give the fierce winds.

She keeps in touch with neighbourhood goings on by regularly reading the local newspaper, the "*John O'Groat Journal.*"

She uses Mey when she really wants to get away from everything . . . ceremony, noise and bustle — and even family.

She puts on old clothes and wellies for walks around the moors or along the shoreline, singing to the seals — though she rarely forgets to fling the odd string of her famous pearls around her neck, no matter how scruffy she's looking.

When she is in residence she can go about the countryside quite freely, for the Caithness folk welcome a fellow countryperson with a quiet, natural warmth which does not intrude upon her privacy. She will chat with all and sundry during shopping expeditions in Thurso. She often walks on the cliffs and sands, watching seals at play. She gathers shells from the beach and heather from the moors.

The occasional warmth from the Gulf Stream allows flowers and fruit to flourish inside the garden, which has been cultivated to perfection. On a long summer's evening, when it stays light till almost midnight, she sits on a bench against the walls of the castle and watches the sunset, at peace with the world. The happiest moment every year is the arrival of her daughter on the traditional Western Isles tour in the Royal Yacht, *Britannia*. Other family members come ashore and the day is spent in familiar bliss and fun. As *Britannia* departs, the flashing of lights to and from castle and Royal Yacht are signals between mother and daughter bidding each other farewell.

She likes to have close friends, and her grandchildren with her at the castle. There is room for twelve guests, who will most likely be young people. They and the Queen Mother can enjoy a daily round of mackerel fishing, crab catching, picnics and relaxed, strictly non-dressy dinners, followed by an eightsome reel or two.

With her passion for the open air, she will pull on an old felt hat and a mac, and haul her little house party and her dogs out, rain or shine, even if it means squatting down and eating lunch in a dripping barn.

The Queen Mother cannot escape to Mey as often as she would like, but life in that part of the world is so totally carefree from life in the more sophisticated South.

MEY HAS NOW been in her care for more than a quarter of a century. Eventually it may well pass on to Prince Charles, who shares his grandmother's love for the open Scottish countryside.

On Sundays she goes to morning service in the little whitewashed parish church of Canisbay, and afterwards chats to the minister and the congregation.

At all their holiday homes in Scotland the Royal Family attend church services every Sunday. They do this at Crathie when they are in Scotland, and during their English holidays at Sandringham's little parish church when in Norfolk.

These are the only occasions when it is possible for the public to catch a glimpse of them during their long breaks from public duties.

When staying at Windsor the place of worship to which the family go is one which is not seen at all, though, for it is almost alongside Royal Lodge, in the private part of Windsor Great Park.

This little church outing was begun by George IV, and later, Queen Victoria who gave the church a homely look, with just a touch of a Scottish village kirk.

She had flowering trees and rose-covered fences set around it.

The Queen Mother walks along from the Lodge for morning service at this Royal Chapel of All Saints, while the Queen and Prince Philip and their family and friends drive through the Great Park from Windsor Castle.

The Royal Family occupy a special stall out of sight of the rest of the congregation, which is made up mainly of tenant families, estate workers, and others who have houses on the Windsor lands. Although the Royal Stall is tucked away, the Queen Mother has the habit of peeping around the pillar.

Of all her homes, Royal Lodge is her favourite. She has spent so much time there, over a period of more than fifty years, and the house is crammed with memories.

She begins her days there sitting at her desk in the Octagon Room of Royal Lodge, looking through french windows, down the stone-flagged path bordering the herb garden . . . a view rich with happy memories.

It too is a home that might one day pass to the Prince and Princess of Wales.

She spends much more time there than at any other out-of-town house. The Lodge legally belongs to the Reigning Sovereign, as

Windsor Castle does, but it has for long been the Queen Mother's own place.

She indulges in her hobby of gardening at the Lodge, fiddling with flower arrangements or fussing around the potting sheds. She enjoys managing her own acres. Almost all the gardens of the Royal Houses in London, Windsor, Sandringham, Deeside and Mey have been within her care. She has had a hand in the development of all of them.

Gardening is in her blood, in the tradition of British Kings and Queens who have been makers of lovely homes and fine gardens.

Henry VIII, for example, inspired the splendour of Hampton Court; Charles II brought in French planning to beautify Windsor and St. James's; William and Mary imported Dutch gardens into Kensington and Hampton.

The Queen Mother has planted the appropriately named roses called Elizabeth of Glamis at Windsor, and lemon-scented verbena which she touches as she comes into the back porch.

Her enthusiasm for gardening led her to accept the patronage of the London Gardens' Society. This takes her away from the vast, carefully laid-out acres of palaces and castles to simple back-street homes within the capital. There, the talk is usually about bedding roses and fertilisers, as she shares a cuppa and chat with fellow amateur gardeners. One nervous soul, trying to be on his best behaviour, was astonished when the Queen Mother told him in a matter-of-fact way: "I always find horse manure seems best for roses — don't you?" With such a well-known horsey family about her, the Royal roses should be blooming!

On one of her gardening walks a woman of about her own age wished her a "Happy Birthday" when it was still a few weeks away. The Queen Mother asked how she knew the birthday was due and the woman explained that they both shared the same date — August 4th. The Royal visitor just nodded and said no more. But in the post at that suburban address a month later was a greeting card from Clarence House.

Inside the Lodge she welcomes visitors in the saloon, which is said to be the heart and the showpiece of the house. Five great windows lead to the wide terrace and the views of spreading lawns and woodlands, wide lawns bordered by azaleas and camelias, rhododendrons, bushes and two old cedar trees.

Elizabeth has made it a beautifully homely place. With tasteful comfort, she has furnished the house, making it a bright and welcoming home.

Royal Lodge is a greatly loved retreat, but Clarence House is where she displays another of her pastimes — art collecting. This began when she inherited a number of fine large pictures when she went to live in the house more than thirty years ago.

Now, the paintings, *objets d'art*, trophies and photographs not only reflect her taste, but record a history of her life and that of her family. There are pictures and paintings of her children, grandchildren and great-grandchildren, portraits of her ancestors and painting and photographs of her Bertie.

There are many works showing herself and George VI, but also photographs taken by such illustrious Royal lensmen as Cecil Beaton, Marcus Adams, Lord Snowdon, Lord Patrick Lichfield and Norman Parkinson.

She has taken a great deal of time and trouble to gather paintings and mementos of her own family line, the Bowes and the Lyons. There is a striking canvas in one corridor at Clarence House showing the Tenth Earl of Strathmore on his charger.

Elsewhere, the Queen Mother's Great Uncle Thomas the Twelfth Earl, is depicted in a watercolour mounted in his racing colours. A further link with racing is another ancestor captured in oils, John Bowes of County Durham who had four Derby winners.

Dominating the glass-fronted display cabinets are the racing trophies Elizabeth has amassed over the years, and gifts of china and silver she and Bertie received during foreign tours and on State occasions.

Her taste in paintings is very wide — from modernists to classical. So, mixed together are canvases from such as Sydney Nolan and Paul Nash, together with Sickert, Steers and Sisley.

She set up her household at Clarence House a little more than a year after the death of King George VI, and just a few weeks before the Coronation of her daughter.

Her sitting room at Clarence House, with its silk upholstered furniture and large mahogany desk, is her working headquarters. During a working day that usually begins at 11.00 a.m. and sometimes does not end until 11.00 p.m., the Queen Mother keeps in touch with the 300 or so organisations of which she is president or patron, plans her official engagements, goes through her mountains of mail and maintains an extensive private correspondence. After work, the day is by no means over: social evenings, which can include film screenings, often last until the early hours.

In public she remains as cheerful and as interested in people as she has always been throughout more than sixty years of Royal life. When she flashes the famous smile it is hard to remember that she is 86 years of age.

There have been rumours that the Queen Mother would retire going as far back as 1956, and were so strong ten years later that property prices in Malta soared when it was believed that she was having a retirement home built there. Today she seems as determined as ever to carry on working.

She makes few concessions to her age. She has a firm answer to friends and members of her household who suggest she might cut down on official engagements: "I'm giving up nothing." And she refuses point-blank to disappoint any of the organisations of which she is patron, president, Colonel-In-Chief or merely a good friend. Attempts to persuade her to drop this or that activity have met with rebuff: "But you have chosen the one thing that I really enjoy doing."

On her eightieth birthday, the Queen Mother became an Old Etonian: or to be precise, she was elected an honorary member of the Old Etonian Association.

This birthday tribute, which entitles her to wear the OEA colours of pale blue stripes on black, gave both the Queen Mother and the school much pleasure.

Apart from the long connection of the Bowes-Lyon family with Eton, she had, of course, engaged an Eton master, the late Sir Henry Marten, to teach our present Queen history. She herself had been a regular guest over the years at boys' concerts and plays. Each February, too, she invites the Eton College Beagles to a lawn meeting at Royal

Lodge, an occasion noted for both the warmth and generosity of her hospitality.

The task of welcoming her to the Old Etonian Association fell to its president. As it happens, the office was held by her private secretary, Sir Martin Gilliat.

One of her favourite activities is salmon fishing. And here she *has* made a concession. For these days she is a fair weather angler. When the river is near freezing the Queen Mother no longer wades in up to her waist after the salmon.

Although, rather like the fish, Her Majesty can sometimes be caught . . . by tourists.

A coachload of them spotted her wrestling with a salmon and converged on the opposite bank.

The protective gillie tried to shield her from the unexpected guests and also catch the salmon's tail at the same time as she brought it in.

Ahh . . . it proved too much and the fish slipped from his grasp and got away. Despite it all the Queen Mother returned the smiles and waves of the tourists and accepted the loss more graciously than many other anglers might have done.

Freezing rivers apart, there have been other minor adjustments to her public calendar. It's unlikely, for instance, that she will undertake a long and distant Royal Tour ever again much, perhaps, to the dismay of the press.

Journalists who cover Royal events tell many stories of the Royal Lady they think is "fabulous." To them the word radiant should have been created specially for her.

For example, while waiting with Pressmen one day at Glen Muick for a Highland regiment to appear from a Cairngorm march, she told them: "Isn't it a beautiful view," and then handed one of the photographers part of her packed lunch — a banana!

WHEN THE QUEEN celebrated her Silver Jubilee the Lord Mayor of London spoke of her being "blessed with a mother whose special place in the hearts of the people has seldom, if ever, been equalled in our long history." At a more simple level, an American Army Sergeant she met once referred to her as "a swell gal." One of her entourage put it another way when he said: "No one comes any better."

She has a great love for Scottish music and dancing. Jack Sinclair, whose band plays for Royalty on Deeside, said the Queen Mother "looks 30 years younger when she is dancing. She hardly misses a dance."

A close acquaintance of hers said: "The thing that no one can understand, of course, is where she gets all her energy from. She is astonishing. But much of it must stem from her upbringing, when she walked the farm with her father in all weathers. She's happiest now, I believe, just walking the shore near Mey, the wind blowing, wearing wellingtons and a wool hat and warm clothes."

Mey is the one place where the gracious lady, who has been "on parade" for nearly 45 years, cannot exactly let her hair down, but at least be "ordinary." She can walk where she likes, chat to neighbours, discuss the crops without anyone watching her every move. And she can make — and even listen — to the odd joke. She likes jokes.

She has never been known to lose her temper in public. The only time she really blew her top was when an American newspaper claimed she was about to remarry. The object of her affections was supposed to be her then 74-year-old treasurer, Sir Arthur Penn. Her Press Secretary announced that it was "complete and utter nonsense." Privately, he added that she had been in such a blinding rage that the language she used was too blue to repeat.

One of her idiosyncracies these days is to insist on complete quiet in Clarence House after 8.00 p.m. Come eight o'clock and everyone's whispering and walking around on tip-toe. This came to light last year when a party, given at Her Majesty's London home came to an abrupt and rather unpopular stop earlier than the uninitiated guests had anticipated.

The Queen Mother herself was not present, though in residence in another part of the building. The situation was politely accepted and the guests took their leave making their way to their vehicles in the Clarence House courtyard.

Only then did it become apparent to those leaving after eight o'clock quite how strict the rules of silence can be. For they were all required to push their cars — with the help of guards and policemen — some 100 yards into the Mall before starting the engine.

Tory MP Norman St. John Stevas tells a tale about when he was a guest recently at Windsor returning to the library to fetch a book before turning in to bed. The castle was quiet but as he approached the library he could hear the slightly eerie sound of pre-war music. As he entered the room there was the Queen Mother performing a solo foxtrot to the accompaniment of an old 78 gramophone.

On another occasion at Clarence House, the Queen Mother rang for a glass of water late at night. When there was no response she got up and got it herself — passing as she did a sleeping policeman who was supposed to be on guard duty. She pinned a note to his tunic. It read: "*I got it myself, thank you, have a good night.*"

She has kept every outfit she has ever worn. Her cupboards are still crammed with beaded Thirties ballgowns and fur wraps. Sometimes dresses that are ten years old get sent back to her dressmakers with the request, "just add some new little sleeves."

She has a fondness for flowery hats and hates uncovering her wispy, permed hair. Yet she has never been vain enough to have her discoloured teeth fixed.

An example of the charm and wit of the Queen Mother was once given in a little story which Dr. Gunapala Malasekera, the former Sri Lankan High Commissioner in London, used to tell his friends. He recalled that when she visited New York while he was Ambassador to the United Nations she had asked him where his home was in Ceylon. "Negombo, Ma'am," he had replied. On being asked what was the principal occupation of its people, he had answered: "Fishing, Ma'am."

Several years later at a graduation ceremony at London University, it was pointed out that Dr. Malasekera held two degrees from the university. At the end of the proceedings she went up to him and said: "Ah, two degrees. That is because of all the fish you eat in Negombo."

The Queen Mother had a special word for

the Royal Hospital's oldest resident at the Founder's Parade in Chelsea when she called there in the summer of 1986. She paused for several moments to talk to 95-year-old retired Grenadier Guard John Russell, who said: "I have met her about five times now, but every time she is so kind and gentle. She told me I was looking very smart and healthy for my age."

The Queen Mother briskly inspected the 300 parading pensioners and complimented them on their turn-out and bearing. "You have served your country with courage and devotion and set a splendid example for the young Army of today," she told them. Average age of the pensioners on parade was 78. The Founder's Parade commemorated King Charles II, who set up the hospital for old soldiers in 1681.

For the first time in seven years since she was appointed Lord Warden of the Cinque Ports, the Queen Mother braved an overnight stay at the official warden's seat, Walmer Castle, Kent in July 1986.

Until then officials of English Heritage who look after the castle had been unable to persuade her to do so, because the private apartments were so drab. But decorators gave it a colourful new look, and Elizabeth stayed for several days from 18th July as part of the 250th anniversary celebrations for Margate.

She employed her own interior designer. A spokesman said: "The previous wardens have always been men, but the Queen Mother likes her surroundings light, bright and spacious."

According to Lady Longford, the Queen Mother is very sensitive about her height. "She's only 5 ft. 2 ins. and that does aggravate her," said Lady Longford of the little lady who once asked a servant to please look out of a high, heraldic castle window, "and tell me who's arriving because I'm afraid I can't reach."

"That's why she always wears high heels, so you think you're talking to someone of at least 5 ft. 4 ins. — though it's wonderful what she can do to you when she's looking up at you."

According to Lady Longford again: "There's much more to her, but few people see it. Everyone raves about her charm. Few people catch her wit. You've only to look at her portraits to see that.

"A close friend once said, 'She's instant sunshine. When she gets up on a platform it lights up and all her feathers and sequins are part of it.' She is terribly sweet. But she's not the pink sugar most painters make her out to be. She's more like a lovely lemon sorbet, with quite a tangy streak."

Princess Anne said this of her grandma: "Nobody can refuse her anything, so she recruits most of us at one time or another."

Staff at Royal Lodge, Windsor, were once stunned to find the Queen on her hands and knees weeding a flowerbed. As they approached, Her Majesty got up brushing dirt off her skirt and explained: "Well, Mummy couldn't find a gardener."

Prince Andrew got the sharp end of her tongue when he sprayed paint over a group of Pressmen in California two years ago. "If only he had apologised at once he wouldn't have got into quite so much trouble," sighed his grandmother.

Elizabeth likes following the horses. One of her closest friends is Fulke Walwyn, who trains her horses at Lambourn, Berkshire. "She came down to visit us here one Sunday," he says. "I was surprised to see her so soon after a tiring tour of Canada. But she seemed as lively as ever. It must be her wonderful keenness about everything that keeps her young. I wish I knew her secret."

A regular guest at Clarence House, Norman St. John Stevas, thinks "She has the spirit of eternal youth. She may look like a gracious old lady. But she has this extraordinary bubbling, young personality."

SHE DEMONSTRATED how she was still in touch with all going on around her, and still caring for people towards the end of 1985, when the plight of a blind pensioner who lived in terror on Britain's toughest housing estate touched her heart. She offered help to 74-year-old Albert Rawlinson and his despairing neighbours after reading a *Daily Express* investigation into the appalling conditions on the Silwood council estate in South London, where drug-crazed gangs ruled the tower blocks. She was concerned about Mr. Rawlinson whose flat was broken into seventeen times that year. He slept in a chair at night with a hammer at his side in dread of being burgled.

Mr. Rawlinson said: "I hope the Queen Mother comes to see us, but just knowing she is showing an interest has made me feel ten years younger. I can't get a home help here because conditions are so bad, but I'll get down on my hands and knees and scrub the place if she would like to come and visit. I am overwhelmed that the Royal Family should take such an interest in the problems of poor people. We really thought we had no hope. Perhaps I am not alone after all."

The Royal lifeline to the 4,000 residents on the problem estate came in a phone call from the Queen Mother's lady-in-waiting, Ruth, Lady Fermoy.

Lady Fermoy rang the local vicar, the Rev. Malcolm Magee, and told him: "It's terrible people have to live in these conditions. We are particularly concerned about poor Mr. Rawlinson. We would like to do anything we can that might improve the position."

Mr. Magee said later: "I was surprised and delighted. Lady Fermoy said she had rung on the express wishes of the Queen Mother after a copy of the story had been posted to her office by a resident. I suggested a letter of concern to the two councils who control the estate would be very helpful."

During her years of Royal duties she has developed a keen sense of knowing how best to present herself to the public. She ticked off Cecil Beaton, for example, for making her look too glamorous in the pictures he took for her 50th birthday.

Wherever she goes she reciprocates the warmth with which she is greeted. "I love meeting people," she says. "I have met people of every possible kind and it is so easy to get on with them after the first moment, isn't it?" And again: "Nearly everyone is pleasant. When one is eighteen, one has very definite dislikes, but as one grows older, one becomes more and more tolerant, and finds that nearly everyone is, in some degree, nice.

"The only regret one has as one grows older is that things do not matter so strongly."

The Queen apart, the Queen Mother is a runaway victor in any Royal popularity stakes. Her informal, homespun style towards her State commitments over the years has led to a most welcome easing of much of the pompous protocol which surrounded many earlier British monarchs.

She has set an example which has been readily adopted by other Royal ladies like the Princess of Wales, Princess Anne, the Duchess of Kent, the Duchess of Gloucester and Princess Alexandra.

A measure of the public's esteem was demonstrated as early as 1953 when dockers broke a national strike to load her baggage aboard a liner to Southampton. When one of them was asked why, he said: "Because she's the nicest lady in the world."

The theatrical crowd have adored her, too, over the years. She is the star of the evening at any theatre she visits. At one Royal Variety night, the late Maurice Chevalier ended his act by going down on one knee and singing to the Queen Mother sitting in the Royal Box: "You must have been a beautiful baby." The final line he changed to, "'Cos, Majesty, look at you now!"

After more than sixty years as a touring representative of the Royal Family, Queen Elizabeth the Queen Mother still displays a thirst for adventure that seems unquenchable. It was entirely in character that she should choose a flight on Concorde as a special birthday treat on her 85th birthday; her enthusiasm for new experiences is as strong as ever.

During her resoundingly successful tour of Canada in 1985 she was in tremendous form. Not many of her fellow countrywomen a few weeks short of their 85th birthday would even have considered a trip to Canada — yet the Queen Mother packed in an eight-day programme of wearying official appearances that had no visible effect on her health or humour.

The element of sheer fun that accompanied the Queen Mother's tour was nowhere more apparent than in Toronto, where she suddenly decided that she wanted to visit the city's futuristic tower — at 1,815 feet the world's tallest free-standing structure.

Her itinerary had been planned in the minutest detail months in advance, with no mention of any Royal interest in the tower. Yet when the Queen Mother arrived in

Toronto and saw the tower looming over the city, she remembered she had last seen it during a visit eleven years previously when it was little more than a hole in the ground.

The Royal request to visit the observation platform and revolving restaurant near the top of the tower was duly communicated to her Canadian hosts, who scrambled anxiously to oblige.

In 1958 there was a trip down a lane of particularly painful memories. She carried out the tour that Princess Elizabeth and Philip had begun in 1952 because George VI was too ill. She decided to "finish" that journey to New Zealand and Australia.

The Queen Mother's Household checked back to the original draft itinerary, reviewed the file of invitations and subsequent amendments, and discreetly drafted a route, complying with her obvious challenge to herself to go over much of the ground toured with her husband in the early years of her marriage.

In six strenuous weeks she permitted herself only a day free from official duties. She felt that it was what her husband would have wished. Every strategic decision clearly rested on what he would have done. "Well, I made it," she said to Sir George Holland, the first in line to meet her in Canberra. The reference was not to the fatigues of the tour but to her long-standing promise to open the headquarters of the Servicemen's League. "I hope I'll get there," she had reaffirmed, "before I'm in a wheelchair."

Her daily activities were best summed up in an engraved crystal engagement holder given to the Queen Mother by her former private secretary, Major T. C. Harvey when he left her household. It read as follows:

> PLEASURES — A myriad to
>   rehearse! . . .
> The likely horse . . . The lucky
>   'hand' . . .
> The leaping trout . . . The living
>   verse . . .
> The favourite waltz . . . The floodlit
>   dome . . .
> The crowds, the lights, the
>   welcome . . .
> — and (sweet as them all) the going
>   home!

> DUTIES! . . . The emblazoned
>   document . . .
> The microphone, while nations
>   listen . . .
> The moments when the ranks
>   present . . .
> This tape to cut . . . That stone to
>   lay . . .
> Another Veuve Clicquot to christen
> The great bows that slide away! . . .

Her constant interest in how people live was vividly shown when she was taken to see the outside of a mews flat in Paddington. She couldn't go inside she was told, because of a difficult staircase. She swept away the objection and insisted on going up to see the flat as well. There have been many occasions when the timing of the whole tour has been endangered by her interest in going into other people's homes.

Over the years she has retained her freshness and sense of enjoyment. Although *things* are often the same — the ribbon to cut, the stone to lay, the speech to make — *people* are always different, and people are her abiding interest.

She is a fanatic about health, through exercise, and her longevity must in large part be due to the fact that every day, come rain or storm, she goes out. In Scotland she walks for mile upon mile without showing any signs of fatigue.

She has had two serious operations in the past — for stomach problems — but now there is seldom anything more serious than the occasional cold. She would never use a minor ailment as an excuse to put off a public engagement. For her sense of. duty is such that she ignores the odd snuffle and pushes herself to the limit, without ever complaining.

Of-late she had to be rushed to hospital in Scotland because a fish-bone stuck in her throat.

This was not the first time such a scare had worried the Royal Family.

One night in November, 1982, during dinner at Royal Lodge a fish-bone stuck in her throat and threatened to choke her. No help by her family or local doctor brought relief, so she was rushed to a London hospital in the early hours for the removal of the obstruction, under a general anaesthetic. The extraction was smoothly done and the patient "came round" with the resilience of a youngster. Little more than twenty-four hours later, she stepped out smartly dressed and smiling, with a pause and a wave for the multitude of waiting cameramen, nipped into her car and was driven home. Her staff, though accustomed to her resilience, described her as "bubbly, quite amazing."

This incident proved again her strong constitution. But the anxiety and the prayers were a measure of the affection in which Elizabeth is held. Newspaper headlines cried: *"Queen Mum — Emergency Operation"* — and a nation held its breath and waited for every bulletin.

There have been earlier worries for her children. She underwent an appendectomy in King Edward VII's Hospital for Officers in 1964 — and almost immediately afterwards was sitting up and receiving friends, smile in place and face and hair immaculate.

WHEREVER she is, no matter what she is doing, the Queen Mother always finds some moment during her day to indulge in her favourite pastime — horseracing. Such is her love for this traditional sport of kings that she has got a betting-shop style "blower" system at Clarence House, where she can hear the up-to-date commentary on runners, riders and races.

The first newspaper she turns to with her breakfast is *"The Sporting Life,"* and sometimes she arranges for early editions to reach her the night before. She not only studies form, but has her own stable of steeplechasers, which, over 30 years, have notched up nearly 400 wins.

While the Queen is a recognised expert on flat-racing and the breeding of thoroughbreds, the Queen Mother is not only an avid follower of steeplechasing, but also one of the most knowledgeable and popular figures at the many meetings she attends. She loves going to the races, rain or shine. Often she will turn up unannounced, causing a minor

security problem, but as soon as her standard is raised on the flagpole a cheer goes up from the punters, trainers and jockeys alike. She enjoys the company of the racing crowd.

Her interest in steeplechasing began in 1949 when she had dinner at Windsor Castle with Lord Mildmay of Flete, a leading amateur rider who persuaded her to buy a horse. Mildmay acted as her racing manager and he and trainer Peter Cazalet looked for a suitable jumper. They selected Monaveen, a Grand National chaser. In only her second season she had a great success with this and a powerful brown horse, Manicou, which won the race named after her husband, the King George VI Stakes, at Kempton Park. Manicou was put to stud and sired a generation of successful jumpers.

During the early days the Queen, then Princess Elizabeth, and her mother jointly owned Monaveen. The daughter gave up her interest in jumpers, though, after the horse broke a leg and had to be destroyed. The Queen is remembered as being heartbroken and she has never been fond of steeplechasing since then.

The accident happened after the King and Queen and their daughters went to Aintree to see Monaveen run in the 1950 Grand National. He led the field that year until the fence before The Chair, when he blundered badly. His winning chance went, but he finished a creditable fifth. Later that year at Hurst Park, Monaveen attempted to win the Queen Elizabeth Chase for the second time. He fell on the second circuit, broke a leg and had to be put down. The Queen Mother, though very upset at the loss, decided to carry on.

Very soon her colours of blue, buff stripes, blue sleeves, black cap and gold tassel were a familiar sight in the winner's enclosure.

After Manicou, her greatest success in the early days was with an Irish horse, Devon Loch, which she also bought in 1950. He swept to many victories, but his greatest opportunity came in the 1956 Grand National. Second time around at the Canal Turn he was second, and in the long run-in to the winning post Devon Loch drew away and looked as if he was going to win by between 20 and 30 lengths. But 50 yards from the post he fell flat on his belly. His jockey, Dick

Francis, believes that the thunder of applause greeting a Royal winner frightened the horse.

When the Queen Mother commiserated with Francis, now a novelist, she went down to see her horse. "You dear, poor old boy," she said, patting him on the neck. Devon Loch ended his days galloping around the fields at Sandringham.

Over the years she had some remarkable successes, but has never made as much money as she could have done because she doesn't believe in selling off horses when they turn out to be duds or are past their prime. She keeps them for sentimental reasons. As a result, her profit over thirty years of racing amounts to a few thousand pounds rather than hundreds of thousands.

At her peak in the Sixties she had twenty horses in training, but now she keeps just eight jumpers at the Lambourn stables of Fulke Walwyn, who took over after Peter Cazalet died.

Some of her jumpers have cost more than 20,000 guineas. When one of them was beaten in quite a humble race at Folkestone on one occasion by a hurdler that had cost only two hundred guineas she told its owner: "I think you got better value for money!"

One of her traditions when going to Cheltenham races is to pop into Mr. Philip Delaney's shop in Prestbury, Gloucestershire, for a chat. It's something she has done sixteen years running and he usually waits with a box of her favourite mint chocolates. It started on the first occasion in a spontaneous gesture. He threw into the car a tube of Polo mints and a bunch of freshly picked daffodils, spraying the Queen Mother with mud and slime. She didn't mind the mess. "Thank you so very much," she said. "And thank you for the Polos." Mr. Delaney, in time, found he had to move, and sadly told the Queen Mother that, in effect, they "couldn't go on meeting like this."

"Nonsense," she told him. "You must tell me where you are going." The following year the Royal car made a considerable detour, and has done so ever since. Mr. Delaney even lays on a modest red carpet from the door of his village shop.

The dirty daffodils have now become a glorious profusion of the finest flowers that money can buy and the Polos have become a tray of confection fit for a Queen.

Elizabeth showed her keen sense of humour recently when she named one of her horses after the Very Rev. Fraser McLuskey, ex-Moderator of the General Assembly of the Church of Scotland. The Kirk's view of gambling was likely to set the heather ablaze but the two-legged McLuskey said of the four-legged McLuskey: "It is a great honour."

Towards the end of 1985, however, it was revealed that she had stopped placing bets. "She doesn't bet at all now," said her private secretary, Sir Martin Gilliat, who used to dash off to the betting shop nearest to St. James's Palace to place discreet wagers on his employer's behalf.

The Queen Mother's knowledge goes beyond the racing form books that dominate the shelves in her study. She can spot when a horse is unwell, or if it has a muscle injury. She once called suddenly on the stables of one of her trainers — and immediately spotted a slight swelling on the hind quarters of one of her horses. Until then, even the trainer and his staff had not noticed the problem.

Her knowledge is respected. One of her trainers, Mr. Jack O'Donoghue, said of her: "She knows plenty, she does. By gosh she does. She won't run a horse if the going is not suitable. And she knows what courses suit them. By gosh, she knows as much, if not more, than any other owner."

In 1961 the Queen Mother had the best season for twelve years and got her first hat-trick. Three of her horses won successive races at Lingfield and she finished the season with twelve winners. The same year she gave one of her favourite steeplechasers, Brig-o-Dee, to the Metropolitan Police after he was found not to be suitable for the Queen on ceremonial occasions.

The next year the Queen Mother was top owner with nineteen winners, including Gay Record in the Hunter Handicap, and collected £7,000 in stake money. The same year she also became the first member of the Royal Family to keep a horse in Ireland since King Edward VII. Her horse, Arch Point, entered for the Dublin Horse Show and this was the first time the Royal Family had exhibited.

In October 1964 the Queen Mother notched up her 100th winner with Gay Record's victory at Folkestone and a hat trick there meant she finished the season as leading owner with a total of 106 winners.

"She was up and down like a two-year-old," said a friend. Her grandson Prince Andrew, then four but quite aware that this was Olympic year, asked if his granny would get a gold medal for her triumph.

The Queen Mother has lots of form books and supervises the buying of all her horses. She also takes a close personal interest in their training, going to watch them work out, armed with a pile of sugar and a bucket of carrots. She does not stand on ceremony as far as her horses are concerned and inspected Super Fox in the front garden of her London home, Clarence House. She found one horse, the famous The Rip, in a field behind the Red Cat pub in Norfolk.

By the end of the 1967 season the Queen Mother had owned fifty-one horses and won 160 races worth £74,272. Two years later she got her 200th winner when Master Daniel won at Worcester. Her winnings were up to £95,000.

The Queen Mother has had her share of disasters. In May 1969 Chaser Woodman had a fatal fall at Newton Abbot, and in 1970 Colonsay Isle and Playagain were destroyed within a week of each other. In March 1972 Capstan collapsed and died of a haemorrhage at Wye while leading the field and Game Spirit, winner eight times at Newbury, collapsed and died there in 1977.

But in those years the Queen Mother also had her triumphs. In November 1972 she reached the 250 winner mark with Chaou's victory at Fontwell Park, and two years later Isle of Man and Present Arms won on their first outings. In 1975 Tammuz won the Schweppes Gold Trophy Handicap Hurdle at Newbury, worth nearly £10,000, the most valuable prize she has ever won.

The following year she got her 300th winner with Sunnyboy at Ascot. In 1981 the Queen Mother had seven winners. Special Cargo did particularly well winning the Allenbrook Memorial Handicap Chase and the Kempton Novice Chase.

Major Peter Cazalet was a great friend as well as trainer of her horses at Fairlawne in West Kent. His death seemed to end an era, but then the Queen Mother transferred her horses to Fulke Walwyn at Lambourn.

The Queen Mother is very careful with her horses. If she thinks that the going is too hard, they do not run. If there is a risk, there are telephone calls with her trainers before she will give permission. The Queen Mother is in racing mainly for the love of it, and not the gain. She can wait for the right day and the right going. She takes every precaution to see that nothing goes wrong.

For racing with her has always been a fun thing — not a business. She gets on very well with the jockeys, even the lesser known ones, and often sends them a kind letter or a gift if one of them is injured.

The greatest compliment the jump jockeys could pay her was when they decided to form a cricket team, and asked the Queen Mother if they could use her racing colours. She gave her permission, and also presented them with a cup which is awarded each year to the jockey cricketer making the greatest personal contribution to the side.

Her worries about jockeys was best demonstrated when she told one of them as he was about to mount one of her less predictable horses: "Go out there and look after each other."

SITTING AMONG the guests at the service in St. Paul's Cathedral in 1980 to mark the Queen Mother's eightieth birthday was Lord Snowdon. It was typical of her to have Princess Margaret's former husband at the ceremony, because she always was, and still is, very fond of him. Her daughter Margaret, with her well-publicised goings on, has never had the easiest path through life as far as her emotional involvements with men are concerned.

If ever a girl, then a woman, needed an understanding and compassionate mother to turn to, it has been Princess Margaret, only a few years from sixty years old and still causing raised eyebrows.

Fortunately for her tempestuous daughter and her confused affairs, the Queen Mother must be one of the world's perfect ma-in-laws. There when needed, but never interfering unless asked to do so. All she has ever wanted for her daughter has been happiness. It would be wrong to say that the Queen Mother has a favourite among her two children, but those close to her say that she has always had a softer spot for Margaret Rose.

The mature judgment she has always brought to bear on her younger daughter's activities was first called into use when the Princess, then in her early twenties, fell ecstatically in love with the handsome RAF fighter pilot, Group Captain Peter Townsend, who had been chosen as an equerry to King George VI. As the world knows, it was a love that had a tragic and painful result.

Attitudes have changed since Margaret wanted to marry Townsend, but more than thirty years ago everything seemed to be against them. He was a commoner, he was more than fifteen years her senior, and he had already been married and had children.

The Queen Mother was very fond of Townsend and appointed him to her own household after King George VI died. She is still friendly towards him, and they have met occasionally over the years since the enforced break-up of his romance with Margaret. In his autobiography, Group Captain Townsend says: "My admiration and affection for Queen Elizabeth was, like everybody's, boundless — all the more so because beneath her graciousness, her gaiety and unfailing thoughtfulness for others she possessed a steely will."

Whether or not she tried to use this strong willpower and influence of hers to help Margaret and Townsend find happiness, the Government and other Royal advisers were against the match. Despite the wishes of the Queen Mother and the Queen, the powers that be insisted that the affair had to be ended. He was sent abroad to a forced exile lasting more than two years. The lovers were kept apart, but they continued to exchange letters and phone calls during that period.

A few weeks after Margaret's twenty-fifth birthday, the Queen Mother brought the pair together again at her London home, Clarence House. She left them alone for the evening to see if they could sort out a common sense solution to their problem.

Apart from Townsend's unsuitability as a prospective husband for a Princess, there were also other snags to their relationship. If Margaret went ahead and married the man she so desperately wanted, she would have to renounce all her rights to the Throne, retire from Royal life and forfeit her official "salary" from the Civil List.

Remembering the decision they had to take together, Townsend wrote: "There would be nothing left except me, and I hardly possessed the weight to compensate for the loss of her Privy Purse and prestige. It was too much to ask of her, too much for her to give. We should be left with nothing but our devotion to face the world."

Neither the Queen nor the Queen Mother put pressure on Princess Margaret at this delicate time. They made it clear that she had a free choice. While the mother listened to her youngest daughter pouring out her soul hour after hour, she realised that there was only one real decision to be made — in the atmosphere of those days. With great reluctance, Margaret took the step her friends say she has regretted ever since. On October 31st, 1955, Margaret and Townsend were left alone again by the Queen Mother at Clarence House so they could say a final farewell to each other.

An hour later Margaret issued a statement that referred to such matters as "*being conscious of my duty to the Commonwealth*" and "*mindful of the Church's teaching that Christian marriage is indissoluble.*" It was dressed up in high-minded phrases, but what really mattered was the sentence: "I would like it to be known that I have decided not to marry Group Captain Townsend."

The great romance was over, finished for ever . . . but the pain of parting was softened by the Queen Mother's shoulder always being there to cry on.

Four years later Margaret fell in love with another commoner, fashion photographer Tony Armstrong-Jones. This was a time when photographers did not have the "in" image they have today and there are some in Royal circles who claim that Margaret deliberately turned her back on better connected suitors to defy those who had caused her so much heartbreak earlier.

Margaret and Tony used to meet secretly in a small cottage alongside the river in London's dockland. It became their own special home, where, among discreet neighbours, they used to have close friends around for dinners cooked by the Princess on a small stove.

The Queen Mother knew what was going on and hoped that this second great love of her daughter's life would have a smooth passage. All that she had been denied five years earlier came true for the Princess on May 6th, 1960, with a wedding in Westminster Abbey that had all the traditional Royal trimmings. Margaret adored her husband and began to enjoy the company of his artistic friends, ranging from fashion designers to film stars such as Peter Sellers and Liza Minelli. Their home in Kensington Palace soon took on quite a bohemian air with all-night parties attended by the sort of guests not normally invited to Royal homes.

The marriage went well, even though Margaret was against Tony making a living and career away from Court circles. He was not prepared just to live off his wife — a decision that impressed the Queen Mother, who admired his independence. But after ten years together, and despite both being devoted to their two children, their love for each other began to sour. It became an open secret among their friends that they were spending more time apart than together.

With their son and daughter away at boarding schools, the need to stay as a couple seemed unnecessary. They are both quick-tempered and their rows became too frequent. Lord Snowdon moved out and into a house of his own a mile away, and they began to lead separate lives. In March 1976 the inevitable happened — they announced their splitting up, which was followed by a divorce.

Throughout this time, and since, the Queen Mother stayed in touch with Lord Snowdon, as a guide and sympathetic adviser. She tried to ease the harshness of their breaking up, especially for the children, Viscount Linley, who was fifteen at the time, and his eleven-year-old sister, Lady Sarah Armstrong-Jones.

Lord Snowdon has remarried, but he and the children still go to visit grandma. She has no bitter feelings towards him, and, although still supporting her own daughter during her later romantic escapades, remains what she has always been . . . the ideal mother-in-law.

THE NATION's love for the Queen Mother was no better displayed than on the day of her Eightieth Birthday. It was a day of singing crowds, tributes by the sackful, champagne and roses, surprise presents and gun salutes for the birthday of Britain's Royal gran, who spent most of it at Clarence House.

The crowd that crushed into the narrow street outside Clarence House from first light wanted more than just glimpses of the Queen Mother on her balcony.

They knew that on every other birthday it had been her habit to come out to meet the people. And so they chanted: "We want the Queen Mum!" They sighed when the black gates opened only briefly to let in other members of the Royal Family bearing gifts for her.

Some who had waited for hours to see her come out began to drift away disappointed. Then at 1.15 p.m., a black-uniformed footman flung back the main doors. Thousands held their breath.

Suddenly, Blackie the corgi strolled down the steps and headed straight for the main gate. And behind was the Queen Mother who followed him into the street. The well-wishers forgot their aching limbs and roared with delight. The Queen and Princess Margaret followed their mother out on to the pavement, smiling at the antics of inquisitive Blackie.

Then five-year-old Andy McKeever, on holiday from Northern Ireland, took his cue. He pushed through a burly policeman's legs to rush up to "my favourite Granny" with a bunch of red carnations. Half a dozen other children copied Andy and raced forward with bouquets.

There were so many that the Queen and Princess Margaret had to move in to help their mother carry them away. The tributes and the flowers, thousands of pink Elizabeth of Glamis roses, had poured in through the side door of Clarence House all morning. But it was little Andy's bouquet the world saw that the Queen Mother carried back herself.

Earlier she had awoken to the sound of bagpipes on the lawn in front of her window. Pipe-Major Duncan and Piper De la Spey of the London Scottish Territorial regiment played a special birthday selection.

Three entire upstairs rooms at Clarence House were filled with the presents. Most of the flowers and cakes were sent later to hospitals and charities. The third time the Queen Mother stepped out on her balcony there was a noisy surprise — a fly past by the Central Flying School of RAF Leeming, North Yorkshire, where grandson Prince Andrew was in training. Ten Provost jets shot by forming a perfect giant 'E' for Elizabeth at 2,000 ft.

Only Prince Philip and Prince Andrew were missing from the birthday lunch. But the night before she was joined by the entire Royal Family for a gala ballet performance in her honour at the Royal Opera House, Covent Garden. They saw a new ballet, *Rhapsody*, composed for her by Sir Frederick Ashton.

She told him later it was "the nicest present I have ever had." Then she blew out the candle on a pink and white cake presented to her after the ballet, and cut it.

She did not go straight home but joined the dancers and Opera House staff at their own party on stage with the birthday cake and champagne. Balloons with the message, "*We love you, Queen Mum*," floated around.

Also on her birthday disc jockey Ed Stewart played a record for her at the request of Princess Margaret. DJ Ed received his Royal summons in the morning and spun the Queen Mother's disc on his afternoon show. Her choice was a recording by Birmingham pop group Driver 67 called "Car 67."

Princess Margaret told him that the Queen Mother liked the song because it had a "warm and human story."

He said later: "I met the Princess at a Girl Guide gala and asked her what her mother's favourite record was. Then I inquired if she might like a request for her birthday. The Princess asked for my telephone number and said she would let me know. She told me she knew my programme and said she always listened to me in her bath on Sunday mornings."

Celebrations for her birthday actually began long beforehand. For months before

and afterwards overworked staff at the House were dealing with the avalanches of presents, letters and greetings cards from all over the world.

Three weeks before the day there was a Service of Thanksgiving in St. Paul's Cathedral. She rode there through cheering streets in an open State landau, with the Prince of Wales sitting beside her, on her way from Buckingham Palace through Westminster to the City.

The Queen deliberately placed her mother to the fore. She and the Duke of Edinburgh and the rest of the Family — Princess Margaret, Prince Andrew and Prince Edward, the Gloucesters and Kents with their children — arrived first at the church.

The Sovereign came out and waited on the steps of St. Paul's to greet her mother and then stood back, accepting second place, as Queen Elizabeth stood waving to the crowds. The Queen Mother, dressed in ostrich feathers and sapphire chiffon, was defiantly bare-armed on a day that was distinctly chilly and had many people in overcoats. But she seemed impervious to the cold.

Colonels of seventeen regiments of which Her Majesty was Colonel-in-Chief or Honorary Colonel were among 2,700 statesmen, political leaders, Ambassadors — and just plain, simple folk — in St. Paul's.

The Queen Mother had ensured that invitations also went out to many people who had been in her service and who had become her friends. There were retired gardeners from Windsor and Balmoral, a lady who did the flowers at Clarence House, former footmen, nursery-maids, cooks and pages still in Royal service, secretaries and chauffeurs — and her present staff. The housekeeper and her husband at the Castle of Mey had been brought down to London. Also there was an old lady who half a century before had been the cook at 145 Piccadilly.

The service was interdenominational, with the Moderator of the Church of Scotland reading the lesson and Cardinal Hume, the Roman Catholic leader, saying prayers.

In his address from the pulpit, the Archbishop of Canterbury, Dr. Robert Runcie, commented that the Queen Mother's famous smiling face had borne "its share of dignity which comes from suffering, but which is full of life, affection and cheerfulness and a zest for new things and people . . . Royalty puts a human face on the operations of Government; and the Queen Mother helps us to feel that being a citizen of this country is not just being an entry on a central computer, but is being a member of a family.

"It is difficult to fall in love with committees or policies, but the Queen Mother has shown a human face which has called out affection and loyalty and the sense of *belonging*, without which a nation loses its heart."

The humble and unknown were also not forgotten on her day-of-days a few weeks later. Elizabeth Carr, who was also 80, was among those in the crowd at Clarence House waving to the Royals. The Queen Mother could not have missed great-gran Elizabeth, standing at a special point at the front of a thousand well-wishers. For a moment their eyes met. They waved to each other. For Elizabeth Carr the occasion was too much. She began to cry quietly.

But that was not the end of her birthday treat. Less than an hour later she got a special telegram as she had a champagne lunch in London. It was from the Queen Mother and read:

"Queen Elizabeth the Queen Mother has heard that you celebrate your 80th birthday today. Her Majesty congratulates you and sends you her warm, good wishes for a happy day."

Elizabeth, who lived in a council tower block in Stevenage, Herts, said: "I just cannot believe this is happening to me. I prayed that the Queen Mum would see me in the crowd. She must have known that I was there to send me the telegram. What a wonderful, wonderful woman she is."

AS SHE SITS in the apartments of her London home, Clarence House, in The Mall, she usually refers to her kinfolk at Buckingham Palace as "those along the road". It is among "those" and their offspring that the Queen Mother gets her greatest pleasure these days. She is, after all, not only a grandma but, thanks to Princess Diana and Princess Anne, a great-grandmother. With the children of other Royals also clamouring for her jolly company as well, she is also a very busy grandparent and grand-auntie. But of all of them who lay claim to her time, no one more so than Prince Charles.

He once wrote about the Queen Mother: "I admit that I am hopelessly biased and completely partisan. Ever since I can remember, my grandmother has been the most wonderful example of fun, laughter, warmth, infinite security and above all else, exquisite taste in so many things. For me she has always been one of those extraordinarily rare people whose touch can turn everything to gold . . . Her greatest gift is to enhance life for others through her effervescent enthusiasm for life."

How many grandmas can sip their cocoa in the evenings with that sort of tribute ringing in their ears?

The Queen Mum began to enjoy grandparentage before she was widowed. Because of George's illness, Elizabeth and Philip had to take on so many Royal duties, and this left Charles and Anne in the hands of their grandma. Also, when he was not on duty as a Royal, Philip served abroad in the Royal Navy, and Elizabeth would join him as a sailor's wife. As a result, so much of the early lives of Charles and Anne were spent with their grandmother. They are still incredibly close to her and seek her advice on any major decisions.

When Elizabeth's own children used to visit their grandma — the stern Queen Mary — it was never something they regarded with pleasure. Princess Margaret has said: "Whenever we had to visit Granny . . . we always felt that we were going to be hauled over the coals for something we had done. But we never were." All the same neither Princess forgot "the hollow, empty feeling" their grandmother inspired. Not so these days for the Queen Mum's own grandchildren. They are devoted to her.

It is inconceivable to picture Queen Mary with any one of her grandchildren riding in an open carriage smiling and waving to the crowds, whilst all the time exchanging jokes with her companion to see who would be the first to dissolve in a fit of giggles.

This is what happened in 1981 when, accompanied by Lady Sarah Armstrong-Jones and escorted by the Household Cavalry, Elizabeth drove the short distance from Windsor Castle to the Home Park nearby where, in a public ceremony, she received the Freedom of the Royal Borough.

She bought toddler Charles a set of miniature gardening tools, though they failed to arouse any permanent interest in being a Royal son of the soil. It was she who set Princess Anne well on the road to her most famous pursuit — some think only — horse riding, when she bought her her first saddle. Anne was then four years old.

Although today brother and sister understand and appreciate one another much more than they used to, their differences in temperament were clearly marked during their long stays with grandma. The Queen Mother found Charles the more sensitive of the two — much more ready than his sister to run to granny when he fell over and grazed a knee, or ask for her support when he and Anne quarrelled. Anne was a bossy little creature, so grandma had to take great care to make sure Charles grew out of his shyness and gained self-confidence.

As the time came round to choose a school for Charles, both the Queen Mother and the Queen were against the rigours of Gordonstoun, a move strongly favoured by Prince Philip, who saw in this spartan life in the north of Scotland a means of toughening up this sensitive lad. When Charles expressed doubts about the school, his father was quick to take advantage of his affection for the Queen Mother by pointing out: "It's near Balmoral. And your grandmother goes up there to fish. You can go and see her."

During his early days at Gordonstoun Charles was particularly grateful for the proximity of the Queen Mother, for she very soon realised how lonely and homesick he was. On visits to her at Birkhall, on the Balmoral Estate, the Queen Mother offered sympathy, gave her grandson the sort of food he liked — and cheered him up. They have always had a relationship that seems more intimate than other grandchildren. Even when he was at school in Australia and feeling a little lonely, the Queen Mother went fishing with him for a few days in the Snowy Mountains.

Charles reminds her of her late husband ... she sees something of the late King's sensitivity to other people's thoughts and feelings in him. A great bond has developed between them. So much so that wherever he is travelling in the world, he sends a steady stream of letters to "grannie" sharing his experiences. She loves to hear all his news, to see how he's looking and make sure he's not overdoing things.

She once said: "He is a very gentle boy, with a very kind heart, which I think is the essence of everything." They make one another laugh and find it the easiest thing in the world to talk to each other non-stop.

Although they are not as close, Princess Anne still stays in regular contact with her grandmother. After telling her mother, Anne phoned the Queen Mother to let her know that she was expecting her first baby. Great-grandma was delighted when Master Peter Phillips was born on November 15th, 1977. "This is one of the happiest days of my life," she observed then.

Princess Anne and Captain Mark Phillips were brought together in the first place by the Queen Mother. This happened when grandma went to a reception in the City of London for members of the successful British equestrian team that had just returned from the 1968 Mexican Olympics.

The Princess had just started getting involved in the strenuous eventing side of riding, so she happily accepted her grandmother's suggestion that she should go along with her to meet some of the experts. And of course among the guests 18-year-old Anne was introduced to was a dashing young Army officer, Lieutenant Phillips, a reserve rider with the team. Mark, who was twenty at the time, and the young Royal discovered they had a common interest — horses. But over the next few weeks, at competitions up and down the country, they were attracted to each other and fell in love. Five years later, at a family get-together to celebrate the 50th anniversary of the Queen Mother's wedding, the Queen proposed her mother's health at a dinner with a speech said to have been "charming, succinct and just right." Amidst the happy babble of well-wishing, Prince Philip rapped for attention and announced his daughter's engagement to Lieutenant Phillips.

Elizabeth was called on immediately to help out with the arrangements. The future in-lawns, Mr. and Mrs. Peter Phillips, were guests in London and at Birkhall during the summer, coming up from their country home in Wiltshire, and received the benefit of her deft guidance through the totally unforeseen problems of a Royal Wedding.

The Queen Mother gave Anne an aquamarine and diamond tiara, among other gifts, and two years after the wedding, indeed when the couple had outgrown their Army home at Sandhurst, she went on several house-hunting excursions for them.

But no one is ever likely to replace Charles in the Queen Mother's affections, although she seems equally proud in the company of her next eldest, Andrew, now the newly-wed Duke of York. She has seen him grow up from being a mischievous toddler to a dashing and brave Naval officer, and now a husband who seems to be taking a more responsible view of life.

The quiet Prince Edward, less flamboyant than his elder brothers, impresses his grandma by being the "brains" of the Buckingham Palace branch of the family.

The Queen Mother has six fully-grown grandchildren, three great-grandsons, one great-granddaughter and many grand-nieces and grand-nephews. There is Lady Helen Windsor, the daughter of the Duke and Duchess of Kent, and Lady Helen's brother, George, the Earl of St. Andrews, who is one of the most academically brilliant of the Royal Family. At twelve he won a scholarship to Eton — the first "Royal" ever to become a King's Scholar.

The Queen Mother has grown close to her grandchildren by keeping up with the times. She likes to be in touch with the latest trends, whether in education or pop music. She learns from "my young people," as she calls her grandchildren, and they in turn find her tolerant of their ideas.

They bring her presents that they have made themselves — a piece of wood furniture from David Linley, a piece of pottery from Andrew when he was at Gordonstoun. Lady Helen Windsor, an accomplished pianist, and Lady Sarah Armstrong-Jones

have also developed her knack of mimicry.

James Ogilvy, Princess Alexandra's son, just over a week older than Prince Edward, has the same nervous energy as his father. The Ogilvy children, James and his sister Marina, have a special place in the Queen Mother's affections because of their father being the second son of the 12th Earl and Countess of Airlie.

In her widowhood it has been a great consolation to her that she has such a fine family of young folk gathered around her. All different in character, all leading lives that are exciting in their various ways. The late Prince William of Gloucester once said: "If I let myself down — say I got into a mess of some sort — my first thought would be that the Queen Mother would feel I had let her down."

She is proud to be in the company of Andrew, the teenage heart-throb. She saw him grow up from being a mischievous toddler to a roving-eyed young man. She spotted a touch of the Duke of Windsor in him.

When the Queen Mother looked around for a suitable bride for grandson Charles, she eventually found her right under her nose — Lady Diana Spencer. The Spencers, their family split by the trauma of divorce, had by then moved to their ancestral home, Althorp in Northamptonshire. It was Diana's older red-haired sister, Sarah, thought at the time to be a flame of the Prince's, who eventually introduced the two as they stood in a muddy ploughed field. Charles had come to Althorp for a day's hunting and he recalled later thinking at the time, "What a very jolly, amusing and attractive sixteen-year-old." Although he would meet her on a number of other occasions, it would be three years before the courtship really began.

The Queen Mother had been a frequent guest during Diana's childhood when the Spencers lived near Sandringham, and had often watched her play with her other grandchildren, Prince Andrew and Prince Edward. Ruth, Lady Fermoy, was the Queen Mother's lady-in-waiting and Diana's grandmother.

A perfect match that delighted Elizabeth.

The speculation about Charles as a suitor ended at eleven o'clock on the morning of

February 24th, 1981. Queen Elizabeth had just arrived at the dais, in the ballroom of Buckingham Palace, to carry out an Investiture. The Lord Chamberlain, Lord Maclean, stepped forward and read this statement:

"The Queen has asked me to let you know that an announcement is being made at this moment in the following terms:

"It is with the greatest pleasure that the Queen and the Duke of Edinburgh announce the betrothal of their beloved son, the Prince of Wales, to the Lady Diana Spencer, daughter of the Earl Spencer and the Honourable Mrs Shand Kydd."

Diana's credentials were impeccable. She had been born just a stone's throw from Sandringham. Her lineage stretched back to the reign of Charles II in 1630. Her family were distantly related to the Royal Family and her father, Edward, the Eighth Earl of Spencer, was a very close friend of the Queen and Prince Philip.

With the romance of Charles and Diana, the Queen Mother found herself in a new role she thoroughly enjoyed . . . chaperone and guiding hand to a new future Queen.

Diana's second day as the future Princess of Wales must nevertheless have been quite a shock to a teenager used to complete freedom. It gave her a foretaste of the way the rest of her life would be mapped out now both as Princess and, one day, Queen.

She woke in what was to be her new home for the next five months of her engagement, the spare bedroom in Clarence House. Outside she could hear the sound of hobnailed boots ringing on the cobblestones as a soldier wearing a bearskin and scarlet jacket, his rifle sloped on his shoulder, paced backward and forward in front of the house's black wooden gates.

On the other side of the house one of the special squad of uniformed metropolitan policemen guarding the Queen Mother was on duty, sitting in a small green hut.

A uniformed footman brought Lady Diana tea on a silver salver. The teenager was more used to getting up and making instant coffee for herself in the kitchen of her bachelor-girl flat in Coleherne Court, Fulham. There were a few raised eyebrows among the Clarence House staff later as the Prince of Wales's lady brought a touch of teenage style to the Royal Household by coming down to breakfast with the Queen Mother dressed in a pair of her favourite jeans and a sweater. Not that the Queen Mother noticed.

She made Diana feel completely at ease as her breakfast companion. And over the next few months the Queen Mother began to share a lifetime's experience of public service with Diana, preparing the teenager for the role she would have to play in society. The rest of the Royal Family soon began to spot the similarities between the girl Prince Charles picked for his bride and his much-loved granny.

Both were sweet-natured but strong; both the youngest daughters of earls, and a rapport with children, wild animals, and Press photographers — in that order! Over the difficult six months of her courtship, constantly pestered by cameramen, Diana remained patient, cool and polite. While Charles and even the Queen lost their tempers with the constant attention, Diana, with Elizabeth's help, remained calm. On the Queen Mother's eightieth birthday, Fleet Street photographers spent their beer money on a beautiful china bowl and huge bunch of flowers for their favourite Royal camera subject, the Queen Mother.

THE FLEET STREET men adored her and had started to like Lady Diana in the same way, especially as the previous evening on her way into Clarence House she had especially turned to give them a wave — and a first-class news picture at the same time.

It was Elizabeth who showed Diana how to develop her own kind of regal wave with her head held proud. She was no longer the shy girl so often photographed on the pavement outside Coleherne Court.

On the evening of her second day as a Royal fiancée, Lady Diana dined with the Queen Mother again, as Royal Household staff wrestled with the problem of how to address her. "We used to call her 'Miss Diana'," said one of the staff. "But now all that has changed and we are not quite sure how to address her. She's much too young to call 'madam.' Perhaps she will let it be known how she want to be addressed." In fact, the more relaxed "Miss Diana" continued to be used.

Diana didn't see her fiancé that night; he was in Hampshire on one of his fixed engagements, dining with officers of the 2nd King Edward VIII's Own Gurkha Rifles as their Colonel-in-Chief. The couple wouldn't meet again for the next two days as the Prince carried out his diary of engagements. Meanwhile the Queen Mother held her hand.

Over the next four weeks Diana and Charles, discreetly watched and cosseted by the Queen Mother, snatched as much time together as the Prince's diary would allow, for they knew they faced yet another long, lonely separation. Buckingham Palace released details of a long foreign tour for the Prince — this time to the other side of the world. Charles was to fly off on March 29th to Wellington, New Zealand, then on to Australia, Venezuela and the United States. He would be away six weeks. Grandma's shoulder to cry on became even more important.

On March 3rd they named the day — July 29th. The place — St. Paul's Cathedral. It was the first Royal Marriage ever to be held there.

In St. Paul's the Queen Mother had pride of place with the Queen and the Duke of Edinburgh in three ornate chairs. On the return journey to Buckingham Palace, no burst of cheers was louder than the one which greeted the Royal grandmother, who had Prince Andrew with her in the landau.

By 1980 Elizabeth had become quite used to the excitement of members of her family getting wed.

In June 1961 there was the wedding of the Duke of Kent to Miss Katharine Worsley in York Minster. The Queen Mother's hectic programme that day was "**10.00 a.m.** Leaves Clarence House by car. **10.15** Leaves King's Cross by train. **1.45 p.m.** Arrives York. **2.00** Arrives York Minster. **3.30** Drives to Hovingham. **4.45** Leaves by car. **5.50** Her plane takes off from Linton airfield. **7.11** Arrives London Airport. **7.13** Takes off by helicopter. **7.30** Arrives Buckingham Palace. **7.34** Arrives Clarence House. Dress: ice-blue coat and feathered hat. **8.45** Leaves by car.

Dress: crinoline, white furs. **8.58** Arrives Covent Garden for gala performance. **12.05 a.m.** Leaves Covent Garden for home." Quite a time for a 60-year-old, as she then was.

Then there was the marriage two years later of Princess Alexandra of Kent to the Hon. Angus Ogilvy. This was of special interest to the Queen Mother, because it meant that the noble families of four castles in Angus, Glamis, Cortachy, Kinnaird and Brechin, in an area of only some seventy square miles, were now linked with the Royal House.

Princess Patricia of Connaught had married the son of the Earl of Dalhousie, Princess Maud of Fife the son of the Earl of Southesk, the Duke of York the daughter of the Earl of Strathmore (Elizabeth herself) and Princess Alexandra the son of the Earl of Airlie.

It linked in marriage a family which had long been in Royal service. Mabel, Countess of Airlie, was lady-in-waiting to Queen Mary for more than fifty years. It was while staying with her that Princess Mary had made one of her first visits to Glamis. The Countess was the first to know of the romance between the Duke of York and Lady Elizabeth Bowes-Lyon. Mr. Angus Ogilvy's father, the Earl of Airlie, had been appointed Lord Chamberlain to Queen Elizabeth in 1937 and by the time of the wedding he had completed over a quarter of a century in this post.

The least extravagant Royal Wedding that the Queen Mother has attended was that of her nephew, Prince Richard of Gloucester, as he then was, to Birgitte van Deurs, a Danish lawyer's daughter. The wedding took place in the tiny 13th-century village church near Barnwell Manor, ancestral home of the Gloucester family in Northamptonshire, and was a compromise between the traditional English wedding and the Danish one which is supposed to be "smaller, jollier and more intimate."

Two months after the wedding, Prince Richard's elder brother, the 30-year-old Prince William of Gloucester, was killed in a flying accident, and Prince Richard inherited the title Duke of Gloucester.

The first Christmas at Windsor following her grandson's wedding proved to be a very special one for the newlyweds — and the Queen Mother. In the middle of the festivities, Charles and Diana let out of the bag the news that she was pregnant. Royal granny was to have another great grandchild.

Until Princess Anne changed the pattern, Royal babies had always been born at Buckingham Palace. Diana's sister-in-law decided to go into the private wing of a public hospital to have her first child, Peter. Since then, the Lindo Wing of St. Mary's Hospital, Paddington, in one of London's less fashionable districts, had become the regal birthplace . . . mainly because of the expertise on hand among the country's finest So it was to St. Mary's that Diana went to have the Queen Mother's latest grandchild, Prince William of Wales on the longest day of the year, June 21st, 1982.

Prince Charles and Diana chose August 4th, the Queen Mother's eighty-second birthday, for William's christening. It took place at the Palace and while posing for official pictures William became bothered by the bright lamps and soon he was howling inconsolably. He was held in turn by grandmother and great-grandmother; and the loud cries did not stop until his mother popped her little finger into his mouth.

Eighteen months later on, February 14th, 1984, Buckingham Palace announced that the Queen Mother could expect another great-grandchild. The Princess of Wales' second child, Henry Charles Albert David, was born on the morning of Saturday, September 13th 1984. "He will be known as Harry," said a Palace spokesman.

The Queen Mother's second grandson, Andrew, was the first child born to a Reigning Monarch since the birth of Beatrice to Queen Victoria, 103 years earlier. He eventually fitted in with his father's plans for a more robust upbringing than Charles. One of the results was an eagerness for a Service career. He became a Naval helicopter pilot and, as we all know, he went with his ship to fight for the liberation of the Falkland Islands.

But perhaps his first taste of explosives came during his gay-blade days when he once had a car "blown up" by the police outside the Queen Mother's home. In his haste to show off his gleaming new acquisition to his grandmother Andrew had parked it outside Clarence House and slipped in through a side door without being spotted by the duty policemen.

Bomb squad officers were alerted to a suspiciously parked locked vehicle, and then wires were seen inside (they led to Andrew's radio telephone) a booby trap device was suspected and the car "entered by controlled explosion."

The summer of 1982 gave the Queen Mother many anxious days. She shared the worries of other families with offspring in the Falklands, for Andrew was running the same risks as other pilots. His eventual safe homecoming on the aircraft carrier *Invincible*, was the focal point of a day of family celebrations.

THE AUTUMN OF HER DAYS

AT AN AGE when most pensioners want little more than to put their feet up, the Queen Mother is leading an amazingly active life. Not for her the gentle routine of knitting, watching television and the occasional old folks' outing. Instead she takes on a busy round of engagements, although it has to be admitted that she keeps her diary a little less full than a few years ago. She is a lady who never seems to tire, always showing amazing energy . . . energy that belies her granny years.

To this day she averages three public engagements a week — and doesn't mind anyone of them. And all because of duty, a duty to serve the nation — and, in any case, she gets great fun out of meeting people.

After spending almost sixty years shaking hands with thousands, making speeches, laying foundation stones, launching ships, inspecting troops, attending banquets and touring the world, you would think she has had enough. Not a bit of it.

According to one of her staff: "We have a terrible job keeping her down. She always wants to be off and about doing things. There always seems to be yet another foundation stone to lay . . . a town she wants to visit again . . . or a banquet she fancies taking on because she enjoyed herself so much the last time.

"And, of course, she is so popular with all generations throughout the world that we have to turn down hundreds of invitations every year. It's a pity, but she would push herself to exhaustion if we didn't do this. How she keeps up the pace is amazing, but I suppose she comes from an era when everyone was expected to work hard. The way she puts every ounce of herself into whatever she's doing must shame many of the younger generation today."

All true. As one of her ladies-in-waiting put it: "She is younger than any of us. We can't keep up with her." As she whizzes about at a breathless rate of knots she never appears to be bored, rarely shows she is irritable, even with the most annoying of hangers-on. And through it all that glorious smile is always there!

For a woman who has met so many people in her lifetime of service, you would think that there was nothing new to interest her. Yet she still brings warmth, approachability and sense of freshness to her Royal duties which delights the crowds that clamour to see her.

As the years have gone by and she has developed that image of a cuddly lady in pearls, she seems to succeed, even more than ever, at turning a starchy ceremony into a relaxed get-together. For example, when she was presenting shamrock to the Irish Guards, of which she is Colonel-in-Chief, she could see the humour of all that splendour, the officers in their scarlet, standing there that day in the pouring rain: "I hope your colours don't run," she told them mischievously.

On another occasion, when she was launching a ship, the Queen Mum had to sit in a wheelchair because she had sprained an ankle. The usually fussy group of big-wigs around her cared little that the thousands of shipyard workers and their families could not see her in the chair. The Queen Mother was having none of this. She ignored the advice not to "stretch herself" and limped to the bow of the ship for the launching: "It doesn't hurt too much and I'm still not so old that I can't walk, gentlemen," she informed them solemnly.

She is eager to tackle anything that is different. In all her years of sitting in innumerable grandstands, in innumerable countries around the world, you would think she must have seen every sport and activity possible, from tossing the caber to sheep-shearing. But then she heard that she had been invited to the Rugby League Cup Final at Wembley. "I like the look of that — I've never tried that before," she told her staff. So off she went to her first Rugby League game and, by all accounts, enjoyed herself!

Children adore her. She makes a point of seeking them out and always chooses the right words to say to them. Take the time when one little lad asked her if it was true that her daughter was Queen? She told him, matter-of-factly: "Yes, isn't it exciting?"

She is associated with more than 300 organisations from the Aberdeen Angus Cattle Society, via the Royal School of Needlework and the Bar Musical Society, to a small group of neighbours in Scotland, the Birkhall Women's Institute. But one of her favourite interests was London University.

She had been Chancellor since 1955, and over the years kept more than 200 engagements with them. She liked going among the students because it kept her in touch with the attitudes of young people.

She was very proud of "her" centre of learning. In a speech she once referred to it, with a hint of a smile, when she said that "the Commonwealth is a loose association of states held together by the University of London." That went down well . . .

Generations of students, many of them full of left-wing republican ideas, have taken her to their hearts. They were always inviting her along to the Students' Union and indeed made her a life member years ago. At their dances she gamely took the floor with escorts who were more used to disco hip-swinging rather than formal waltzes. She once reassured a stumbling president of the union who was having great difficulty putting his feet in the right place: "Don't worry, you haven't knocked my tiara off yet."

God bless her sense of humour. Over the decades she has needed it. Here are some examples. Once on the deck of the liner Queen Elizabeth she was stopped by an American who asked: "Excuse me, but I know your face."

"Oh yes?"

"You advertise something. Now what is it?"

"Oh, it would be too unprofessional to tell you."

Major Donald Neville-Willing was on the same ship. "We had the Marchioness of Winchester on board, an Indian lady. Every time she saw the Queen Mother she sank down in a flood of saris, in the cinema, in the lounges. And of course the Queen Mother had to respond.

"In the end a lady-in-waiting came with a note: 'Would it be possible for the Marchioness to curtsey just once a day?'"

He remembers one religious service on board. "The ship had run into rough weather and the captain read out a message from the Queen Mother, that because of bad weather the congregation need not rise for hymns.

"But when the hymns came it was typical of her that she herself rose. Then she looked to her left and very slowly all the people on her left struggled to their feet. Then she looked to her right and all the people on her right stood up. It was one of the funniest things I've seen."

An old friend of Sir Norman Hartnell tells a story that the Queen Mother told him once: "I hear so much about your place in Windsor. I'll drop in some time."

"It made him ill with worry for years. He knew she loved these enormous Scottish teas and so he filled a cupboard with cakes and biscuits to be ready. The next time, she'd wave her hand: 'I haven't forgotten.' And he'd rush off to his cupboard. When the cakes got mouldy he gave them to his friends.

"Terrified him for seven years, though she meant it kindly. I've never had so many cakes in my life."

She showed her sense of humour once recently when she persuaded guests to take part in an after-dinner game at Royal Lodge, Windsor. Her Majesty decided they should play indoor point-to-point — without the horses. Her distinguished guests were required to circle the room on all fours "jumping" over strategically placed cushions. One slowcoach was encouraged to go faster by the Queen Mother "whipping" him with a furled napkin.

On another occasion, when Lord and Lady Carrington were present at Windsor Lodge, the Queen Mother got guests to dance a Highland reel after dinner, having herself placed an appropriate record on the gramophone.

At the end of the reel the dancers were surprised when their hostess announced that she was going to take the salute. They were required to line up and march past her, saluting as she stood to attention returning the gesture.

She has a special trick to change the subject if she finds the conversation of a table companion boring or embarrassing. She pretends to be foxed by the workings of the twist-and-grind pepper pot and has thus to be rescued, diverting the topic.

THE QUEEN MOTHER is the head of orders of chivalry, holder of many honorary degrees, and a Master of the Bench of the Middle Temple. Among hospitals, churches, charities and assorted societies which have her patronage, there are the Church Army, the Bible Reading Fellowship, the College of Speech Therapists, the British Home and Hospital for Incurables, the Injured Jockeys Fund, the Grand Military Race Meeting, the Royal College of Music, the Keep Britain Tidy Group, and the Women's Institutes of Windsor, Sandringham, Crathie and Birkhall.

Other organisations she is linked with range from major institutions like the National Trust to smaller, personal favourites like the Dachshund Club. She is Colonel-In-Chief of eight regiments or service units in Britain and ten more around the Commonwealth, Commandant-In-Chief of all three Women's Services and the first female Lord Warden of the Cinque Ports.

Her year has developed a settled pattern. March means Badminton, April a week at Windsor. June (an especially busy month) Royal Ascot, Trooping the Colour and the annual Garter ceremony at Windsor. In late

July, just before her birthday, she bases herself at Sandringham and visits the King's Lynn Festival. August, in her widowhood, has become synonymous in the Queen Mother's mind with the Castle of Mey.

There are three dates in the Queen Mother's diary which her staff know to keep free each year. These are the days she withdraws from her public duties to spend a poignant few hours in the privacy of her memories. The 26th of April is the anniversary of her marriage to Albert in 1923; the 14th of December was his birthday and the 6th of February the date of his premature death. They are all anniversaries of which she shuns any public commemoration.

The Worshipful Company of Gardeners send her a bouquet each April. In February, usually at Windsor, she prays alone in the private chapel there.

If spending the day at home, she will often entertain either family or friends to lunch. Otherwise, she will usually share a light snack with members of her household, after a drink or two, perhaps, of her favourite tipple — gin and tonic.

Sometimes at Mey she will come in from fishing, wearing green wellies, and sit watching TV with the staff.

Her staff at Clarence House marvel at the manner in which she manages to follow many activities, and to thrive on them — the travelling, the concert, ballet and theatre dates, the racegoing, the collecting of pictures and antiques, the walking, the fishing, the devotion to dogs, the interest in gardens, the reading, letter-writing, telephoning, family gatherings, and then still finding time to relax.

To keep up with her commitments she is frequently an airborne grannie. She enjoys flying and makes good use of helicopters to save time and to allow her to cover several engagements in a day.

She once flew by "chopper" to Northern Ireland to see her serving soldiers, the Queen's Dragoon Guards, of which she is Colonel-in-Chief. A few weeks later, when her helicopter had to make an emergency landing on to the grass in the middle of Windsor Great Park, she marched off to find a small fixed-wing aircraft to give her a lift to one of her Cinque Ports "dates" in Kent.

THERE HAS never been an historical precedent or constitutional position in the British Monarchy for a "Queen Mother". It has been Elizabeth of Glamis' own strong character and her obvious liking for the role that has established her position at Court and gained her universal acceptance.

Her undoubted strength of character has made her a vital support to her daughter — especially at the beginning of Her reign — and over the past 33 years.

The Queen Mother has earned the love and affection of millions through her unfailing public duty that never shows any sign of slackening. She is still among the busiest of her family.

All a long way in time from the day her husband died, when she picked herself up and got on with her life.

Her doctor said at the time. "If only she could break down. This incredible self-control will take its toll." Fortunately it didn't.

On her 85th birthday The Times paid the following generous tribute to the Queen Mother: "It would have been tragic if, after the death of her husband, she had gone into retreat as Queen Victoria did. Instead, galvanised apparently by a visit at Balmoral from Churchill and inspired no doubt by her own personal philosophy that 'work is the rent you pay for life,' she thrust herself back into public engagements, in the best sustained supporting role the Royal Family has ever produced, after just three months.

"The nation loves her because she learned the art of being Royal without losing the common touch."

Some say that she is the Royal Family's greatest actress. Cecil Beaton once observed; "Of course, there is something of the great actress about her. In public she has to put on a show which never fails."

Only an actress? If so she has spent nearly seventy years "on stage" without ever fluffing her lines or being upstaged by anyone else on the scene. No critic has ever attacked her, for her reputation is impeccable among all of us.

She once said; "It is hard to know when not to smile." Those of us who are her fans are looking forward to her ninetieth birthday. Long may she keep smiling.

HER LIFE AND TIMES ...

Here are some of the major events that happened in her lifetime and have affected our lives . . .

1901 — Queen Victoria dies.

1902 — Boer War ends.

1903 — First powered flight by Wright Brothers.

1906 — Emmeline Pankhurst launches militant campaign for women's suffrage.

1907 — Robert Baden-Powell founds Boy Scout movement.

1909 — Louis Bleriot makes first cross-Channel flight.

1910 — Labour Exchanges are established in Britain. Florence Nightingale dies.

1911 — Norwegian explorer, Amundsen, reaches South Pole.

1912 — SS Titanic strikes iceberg on maiden voyage — 1,513 die. Robert Scott dies at South Pole.

1914 — First World War begins.

1918 — Kaiser William II abdicates. Armistice is signed.

1919 — Albert Einstein's theory of relativity is confirmed. John Alcock and Arthur Brown make first non-stop flight across the Atlantic.

1921 — Irish Free State is set up by peace treaty with Britain.

1922 — Mussolini's Fascist movement marches on Rome.

1924 — Ramsay MacDonald forms first Labour Government in Britain.

1926 — General Strike in Britain lasts nine days.

1927 — Charles Lindbergh flies from New York to Paris in 37 hours.

1928 — Women in Britain win the vote. Airship crosses Atlantic with 60 passengers.

1929 — Wall Street Crash.

1930 — R101 airship crashes in France on first flight to India.

1933 — Adolf Hitler is appointed German Chancellor.

1935 — Sir Malcolm Campbell breaks world land speed record in Bluebird.

1936 — Queen Mary makes maiden voyage in record time to New York from Southampton. Civil War breaks out in Spain.

1938 — Queen Mother launches world's largest liner — the Queen Elizabeth. Austria annexed by Germany. Munich agreement signed.

1939 — Second World War. Spanish Civil War ends.

1940 — Evacuation of Dunkirk.

1941 — Japanese attack Pearl Harbour.

1942 — El Alamein. The Dieppe Raid.

1943 — Allies land in Sicily. Mussolini overthrown and Italy surrenders.

1944 — Allied armies land in Normandy.

1945 — Victory in Europe, and Japan. Hiroshima destroyed by first atomic bomb. Clement Attlee wins General Election for Labour.

1947 — Coal industry nationalised. School leaving age raised to 15 in Britain.

1948 — Berlin airlift.

1949 — Gas industry nationalised. Ten-power conference in London establishes Council of Europe.

1950 — Outbreak of Korean War.

1951 — Festival of Britain opened by King George VI. Conservatives win British general election.

1952 — Britain's first atomic bomb test.

1953 — Eisenhower becomes 34th President of USA. Stalin dies. Hillary and Tensing reach summit of Everest. Coronation of Queen Elizabeth II.

1954 — Roger Bannister first man to run a mile in under four minutes.

1955 — ITV begins transmitting.

1956 — Hungarian uprising.

1957 — First Premium Bond prizes drawn by ERNIE. First satellite launched by Russia.

1958 — Nikita Khrushchev elected to power in Russia. General de Gaulle President of France.

1959 — Fidel Castro takes over in Cuba. Jodrell Bank radios message to America via the moon. First section of M1 motorway opens in Britain.

1960 — John Kennedy elected President of USA.

1961 — Yuri Gagarin makes first manned flight into space. Betting shops open in Britain.

1962 — Marilyn Monroe dies, aged 36. Britain's first communications satellite launched.

1963 — Great Train Robbery. President Kennedy assassinated.

1964 — Harold Wilson becomes Labour Prime Minister. BBC2 Television opens.

1965 — Sir Winston Churchill dies. Ian Smith makes Rhodesian Declaration of Independence.

1966 — England wins World Cup at Wembley. Aberfan colliery disaster — 116 children killed.

1967 — Six-day war in Middle East. First heart transplant in Cape Town.

1968 — Senator Robert Kennedy assassinated in Los Angeles. Russians invade Czechoslovakia.

1969 — Maiden flight of Concorde. Neil Armstrong and Buzz Aldrin first men to land on the moon.

1970 — General de Gaulle dies. Thalidomide disaster.

1971 — Britain goes decimal.

1973 — Britain joins Common Market. Last American soldiers leave Vietnam.

1974 — President Nixon resigns over Watergate scandal. Edward Heath resigns. Labour Government takes office.

1975 — Mrs Margaret Thatcher elected leader of Conservative Party.

1976 — Harold Wilson resigns. James Callaghan takes over. Carter elected President of USA.

1977 — Bing Crosby dies. Freddie Laker starts Skytrain service to New York.

1978 — Cardinal Karol Wojtyla of Poland becomes first non-Italian Pope for 450 years.

1979 — Mrs Thatcher first woman Prime Minister. Shah leaves Iran. Ayatollah Khomeini takes over. Earl Mountbatten assassinated.

1980 — Ronald Reagan elected President of the United States. The Queen Mother's eightieth birthday.

1981 — Prince Charles marries Lady Diana Spencer in St. Paul's Cathedral. Assassination attempts on President Reagan and the Pope. President Sadat and Mrs. Ghandi assassinated. In Poland, Lech Walesa begins his campaign for freedom.

1982 — The Falklands Crisis. The birth of Prince William and the Pope's visit to Britain. Reappearance of the *Mary Rose.*

1983 — Margaret Thatcher re-elected Prime Minister/Neil Kinnock elected Leader of the Labour Party/IRA bombers kill six and injure many more Christmas shoppers at Harrods/Britain's first heart-lung transplant.

1984 — The miners' strike. Ethiopian famine. Spread of international terrorism. Prince Henry born.

1985 — Football violence spreads as fire strikes at Bradford City football ground and fans die in Belgium. The Queen Mother celebrates her 85th birthday.

1986 — Marriage of Prince Andrew and Sarah Ferguson, becoming the new Duke and Duchess of York.

AFTER THE WAR...

Her Majesty Queen Elizabeth poses for the camera in the White Drawing Room at Buckingham Palace.

Her Majesty Queen Elizabeth, The Queen Mother, lovingly cradling her first grandchild, Prince Charles, following his christening in January 1949. The baby Prince wore the Royal Christening robe of white silk and Honiton lace which had been made for Queen Victoria's children. He slept peacefully throughout the proceedings.

His nurse, Sister Helen Rowe, comes to take Charles back to the nursery after the christening. The scene is in the Music Room at Buckingham Palace.

This historic photograph of King George VI and Queen Elizabeth with their grandchildren Prince Charles and Princes
had had an operation for the removal of

...nne was taken at Buckingham Palace on 14th November 1951, the Prince's third birthday. The King's health was failing. He ...ng and was to die a few months later.

Princess Anne's christening was less formal than these official pictures would have us believe. (Left) The
Royal party, with Princess Anne still sound asleep, relaxes in the White Drawing Room and
(above) Queen Mary, now a Great-Grandmother twice-over, reaches for the young
Charles. The Queen Mother's attention is also on the three-year-old.

Their Majesties King George VI and Queen Elizabeth pose for photographs on the occasion of their Silver Wedding Anniversary in the Blue Drawing Room at Buckingham Palace.

A recital from Her Majesty, in the presence of King George, during the photo session to honour their Silver Wedding.

His wife plays and the King turns the pages of her music sheet.

The Official Silver Wedding pictures of the King and Queen were taken in April 1948. After 25 years of marriage, despite the difficult war years and His Majesty's failing health, the Royal Couple are obviously still very happy together. (Above) In the Blue Drawing Room at Buckingham Palace. (Right) The King replies to some of the hundreds of messages of good wishes.

The King and Queen, once again photographed on their Silver Wedding anniversary, are seen here a

e piano. The King looks on as Queen Elizabeth gives a recital of a popular tune of the time: "The Toast."

King George VI and Queen Elizabeth with the Princesses Elizabeth and Margaret look down from the Royal Box
less than 1

ondon's Palladium during the Royal Variety Performance in November 1950. The King, looked drawn and tired. He died
onths later.

The date is August 1951 and Queen Elizabeth and her daughters step out for a brisk walk in the grounds of Balmor
recovered from his rece

following behind is Group Captain Peter Townsend, who was in love with Princess Margaret. The King, although much
out of illness, stayed indoors.

King George VI and Queen Elizabeth at Balmoral with Princess Margaret, who was celebrating her 21st birthday, in the summer of 1951. This was the last time the King was to see the castle.

One of the last pictures taken of King George VI before his death in February 1952. He is seen leaving the aircraft with The Queen and Princess Margaret, at London Airport after saying farewell to Princess Elizabeth and the Duke of Edinburgh prior to their flight to Nairobi. Princess Elizabeth was to return to Britain as Queen.

(Above) Three Queens, Queen Elizabeth II, The Queen Mother and Queen Mary awaiting the arrival of the body of King George VI at Westminster Hall for the Lying-in-State following his death on 11th February 1952. (Right) Lying-in-State at Westminster Hall.

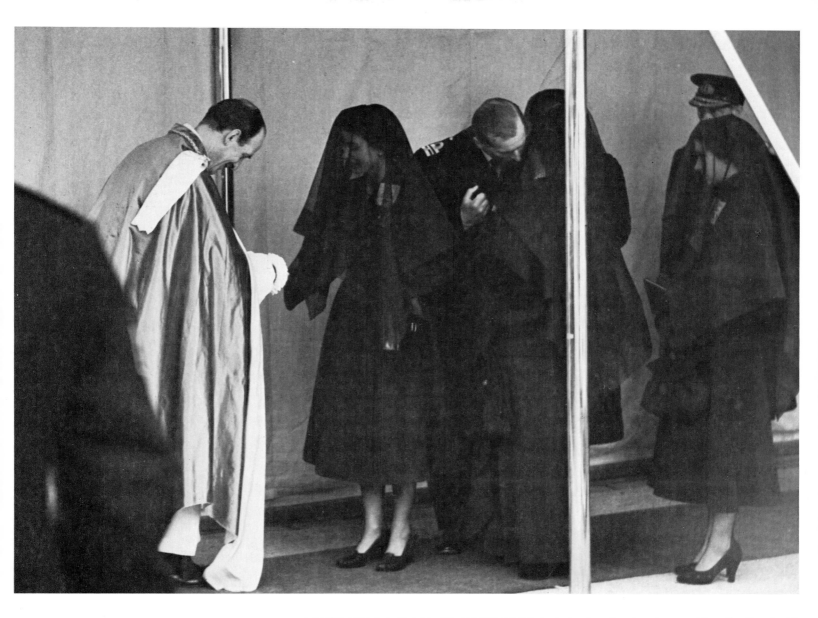

(Top left) The body of King George VI leaving Sandringham for the Lying-in-State at Westminster Hall. (Bottom left) The Royal Cortege four days later passing through the streets of Windsor for the funeral at St George's Chapel, 15th February 1952. (Above) The Queen shaking hands with the Dean of Windsor outside St George's chapel after the funeral service. With them are the Queen Mother, Princess Margaret and the Dukes of Edinburgh and Windsor. (Right) The Queen Mother and the Dean of Windsor. (Overleaf) The Coronation of Queen Elizabeth II at Westminster Abbey, June 1953.

(Left) Prince Charles, pictured during the Coronation of his mother, Queen Elizabeth II, in Westminster Abbey, flanked by Princess Margaret and the Queen Mother who is lending a grandmotherly ear to his questions. (Above) The Queen Mother and Princess Margaret pose for the cameras in the official robes they wore for the Coronation.

Left page and above. Happy Balcony scenes after the Coronation of Queen Elizabeth II on 2nd June 1953. The Royals acknowledge the cheers of the crowds and watch a flypast by the Royal Air Force. The Queen Mother is seen bending to talk to Princess Anne. (Right) An informal picture taken a little later . . . obviously the young Charles is not over-impressed with the pomp and ceremony of the day.

The Queen Mother has always enjoyed a spot of fishing. Here as Duchess of York in 1927 she proudly shows off her catch after a fishing expedition at Tokaann, New Zealand. Such success is difficult to forget and almost 40 years later, Her Majesty returns to the same place to try her luck again (right).

The dedication of a memorial plaque to Queen Mary at Marlborough House in 1967. (From left) Prince Philip, Th
Duchess

ueen, The Queen Mother, The Duke of Gloucester, The Duchess of Gloucester (Princess Alice) and The Duke and
indsor.

211

Queen Elizabeth The Queen Mother, photographed in her London home, Clarence House, where she resides for most of the year. Her Majesty is seen (above) at her desk, cluttered with pictures and memorabilia, attending to her correspondence.

(Left) The Royal Lodge and part of the splendid gardens which were initially designed by the Queen Mother herself. (Above, top) The comfortable furnishings of the Saloon at Royal Lodge, with windows facing out across the lawns, gives some indication of the homely atmosphere which pervades the house and gardens. (Bottom) The Queen Mother's desk at Royal Lodge is in the Octagon Room. The french doors open to a path, laid by King George and Queen Elizabeth, and on to her much loved herb garden.

(Above) Glamis Castle, Her Majesty's Scottish home. Where Princess Margaret was born. (Above right) The Queen Mother's sitting room. (Bottom right) Of all the rooms at Glamis the Great Hall is the most magnificent. Particularly interesting is the fireplace, 13½feet wide and reaching to the spring of the ornate plasterwork ceiling created in 1621.

A view of the Queen Mother's Glamis Castle in Angus, Scotland.

The Queen Mother in the grounds of the Castle of Mey where she keeps a herd of pedigree Aberdeen Angus cattle. Mey was where she sought solace after the death of her husband in 1952.

The Queen Mother always attends the annual Mey Games which take place just along the road from her Castle. She is seen (top) talking to two ladies from Yorkshire who were delighted when she stopped to say hello. The Queen Mother is always asked to present the prizes. This one went to the winning Tug-o-War team, on that occasion her own team from the Castle.

(Above) Always interested in young folk, the Queen Mother chats with young pipers from the Ullapool and District Junior Pipe Band who had travelled from the West Coast of Scotland to perform for her at the Games. (Right) It is not an everyday sight to see a tractor driver resplendent in kilt and medals, but "anything goes" at the Mey Games. Here the Queen Mother is admiring a vintage tractor belonging to Mr Sandy Grant. With her is the president of the local branch of The Royal British Legion, the Games' organisers. The Queen Mother enjoys the informality of the afternoon at the Games and never misses the event.

Mother and daughter meet again at the start of their Scottish holiday. Although they had been apart for only a few days these reunion pictures capture their obvious pleasure at being together again (above and right)

The Queen and Queen Mother at Scrabster on one of the earlier visits of the Royal Family to the Castle of Mey during a trip around the Scottish coast in the Royal Yacht, Britannia.

The Queen Mother with three of her grandchildren: Prince Edward, Viscount Linley and Lady Sarah Armstrong-Jones, after arriving at Scrabster to spend the day at the Castle.

The people of Caithness had never seen the Queen Mother in her beautiful tiara and evening gown until she attended their Jubilee Ball at the Assembly Rooms in August 1977. (Top) Her Majesty dances with the host of the Ball, Lord Thurso who escorts her back to her seat (bottom picture). (Right) Her Majesty, a keen and expert dancer, performing Eightsome Reel, one of the famous Scottish country dances, with other guests.

Her Majesty is obviously enjoying dancing the Dashing White Sergeant, this time with Major Alan Ferrier, of Wick.

Her Majesty enjoying a rest from the dancing and a chat with Sir John Sinclair at the Jubilee Ball.

Dating from 1349, "The Most Noble and Amiable Company of St. George named the Garter" is the oldest
order of Christian chivalry in Britain. The Garter Ceremony, at which new Knights are invested,
takes place at Windsor Castle. A service is then held in the chapel and afterwards the
Queen and her family return in open carriages to the castle. The Queen
Mother is seen here with Charles returning in their carriage.
(See also overleaf).

The Queen Mother always enjoys the ceremony of Trooping The Colour, for it is an opportunity for a great famil

-union. Here they are all together on the balcony of Buckingham Palace watching a flypast by the Royal Air Force.

The Queen Mother tries to attend all the major horseracing events, and the Derby is no exception. She is
seen here enjoying the day with the Princess of Wales, Princess Anne and Prince Philip. (Right)
From the Royal Box there is an excellent view over the course and crowds . . . and a
chance for the Royals to turn the tables to do a spot of celebrity-spotting.

The Queen Mother (above) in the paddock at the Derby inspects the 1986 runners before the race, and watching the horses parade past with Princess Anne, Princess Diana and Prince Charles.

(Left) Cheers for the Queen Mother as she arrives at Royal Ascot in her horse-drawn carriage with Princess Diana. (Above) The Queen Mother pictured on her way back from the paddock to watch the race from the Royal Enclosure.

(Left) The Queen Mother at Ascot, 1986, this time escorted by Prince Andrew and his fiancée, Miss Sarah Ferguson (now Duke and Duchess of York), as she moves through the crowds to the paddock where horses and jockeys assemble before the race. (Above) The Queen Mother and the Queen, who shares her love of horse-racing, in the winners' enclosure after one of their horses had triumphed.

PATRON OF THE ARTS. (Above) The Queen Mother, accompanied by Lord Snowdon, arriving at the Royal Opera House, Covent Garden and (right) taking her place in the Royal Box.

Always glamorous, always welcomed, Her Majesty The Queen Mother, looking delightful in her tiara and diamonds, arrives for the Royal Variety Performance. On one occasion (above) superstars Ken Dodd and Danny LaRue had the honour of being presented to her after the show.

Grandchildren and Great-grandchildren. This happy family group was recorded for the christening of Zara Phillips, second child of Princess Anne and Captain Mark Phillips, in the Music Room at Buckingham Palace in 1981. (Right) Princess Anne's own christening on 21st October 1950. This photograph was taken in the White Drawing Room at the Palace.

During her lifetime, the Queen Mother has of course attended many family weddings. (Top left) The wedding of Princess Elizabeth to Lieutenant Philip Mountbatten in 1947. (Left) Thirteen years later, in 1960, Princess Margaret married Anthony Armstrong-Jones. (Above) Then came the weddings of her grandchildren, the first being that of Princess Anne to Captain Mark Phillips in November 1973

Twenty-five years after the marriage of her eldest daughter, the family gathered for a silver wedding anniversary photograph. This one was taken at Windsor Castle in November 1972. Those present are: 1. The Queen 2. Lord Snowdon 3. the Duke of Kent 4. Prince Michael 5. Prince Philip 6. Prince Charles 7. Prince Andrew 8. the Hon Angus Ogilvy 9. the Duchess of Kent 10. Lord Nicholas Windsor (younger son of the Duke of Kent) 11. the Earl of St Andrews (elder son of the Duke of Kent) 12. Princess Anne 13. Marina Ogilvy 14. Princess Alexandra 15. James Ogilvy 16. Princess Margaret 17. The Queen Mother 18. Lady Sarah Armstrong-Jones 19. Viscount Linley 20. Prince Edward 21. Lady Helen Windsor (daughter of the Duke of Kent).

The Royal Wedding of Prince Charles to Lady Diana Spencer. This picture, taken inside St. Paul's Cathedral
Princess Margaret and Viscount Linley with Lady Diana's father, Earl Spencer, Lady Diana and Prince Charles
at the happy couple but at the page

...hows Her Majesty The Queen, Prince Philip, the Queen Mother and (behind) Princess Anne, Capt. Mark Phillips, ...nd the supporters, Prince Andrew and Prince Edward. But the Queen Mother's attention seems to be directed not ...nd bridesmaids sitting opposite.

255

This family wedding group picture, to commemorate the union of the Prince and

Princess of Wales was taken at Buckingham Palace by Lord Patrick Lichfield.

257

Prince Henry was supposed to be the star at his christening, but big brother William stole the show when it came to the photographs. These official christening pictures show the godparents (standing left)—Lady Sarah Armstrong-Jones, artist Bryan Organ, Gerald Ward, and (standing right) Carolyn Bartholomew and Lady Susan Hussey.

THE EVER-GROWING ROYAL FAMILY

On 23rd July 1986, Queen Elizabeth The Queen Mother attended the wedding of her third grandchild, Prince Andrew to Miss Sarah Ferguson at Westminster Abbey and later joined the newly-weds and the rest of the Royal Family on the balcony of Buckingham Palace, to the delight of the thousands who had gathered outside. (Above) The ever-increasing Royal Family pose for an official wedding picture.

The Queen Mother, who celebrated her seventieth birthday on 4th August 1970, portrayed (above) in one of
the drawing rooms of Royal Lodge, Windsor, her country residence in England. (Right) Her Majesty
is seen here amidst the splendour of the gardens at Royal Lodge. She is a keen gardener
and took on the design of these gardens when she first married. The results,
some 48 years later, are spectacular.

1970—A grandmother several times over, the Queen Mother, looking astonishingly young, posing in the garden on her 70th birthday. (Right) Five years later, celebrating her 75th birthday at Clarence House.

For her 75th birthday Her Majesty invited her favourite photographer, Norman Parkinson, to take the pictures at her London home, Clarence House. These are the results (above and right).

Birthdays have always been a special occasion for the Queen Mother. Here, after a visit to the theatre to celebrate yet another year, Her Majesty is presented with a cake—complete with candles—from the actors. But blowing out the candles and cutting the first slice requires a little help!

THE QUEEN MOTHER ON HER 80th BIRTHDAY

Two charming studies of Her Majesty Queen Elizabeth The Queen Mother with her two daughters Queen Elizabeth II and Princess Margaret, taken on the occasion of her 80th birthday.

St Paul's Cathedral was the majestic setting for the colourful spectacle of the Thanksgiving Service to commemorate the Queen Mother's eightieth birthday in the presence of family and friends (and overleaf).

Her Majesty Queen Elizabeth The Queen Mother chose the beautiful grounds of Royal Lodge, Windsor, for the official photographs to mark her 80th birthday.

Eighty-Three Today . . . and the crowds gather outside Clarence House. The Queen Mother received flowers and cheers when she appeared at the gate. With her, were The Queen, The Prince and Princess of Wales, Princess Margaret and her two children, Viscount Linley and Lady Sarah Armstrong Jones. In the excitement of the moment, one of the Queen Mother's corgis, who was clearly enjoying all the fuss, was almost forgotten and had to be escorted back by one of the policemen outside the gate!

(Left) On her 85th birthday, the Queen Mother posed with four of her grandchildren, those of her eldest daughter, Her Majesty The Queen. The picture caused some controversy at the time—where were her other two grandchildren, Princess Margaret's son and daughter, Viscount Linley and Lady Sarah Armstrong Jones? (Above) The Queen Mother outside Clarence House acknowledging the cheering crowds and (bottom) making her way to the gates of Clarence House to receive some of her presents and cards.

The sun was shining over London for the Queen Mother when she celebrated her 86th birthday at Clarence House. With her to answer to the cheers and good wishes of the crowds who have always gathered outside her house on 4th August were (from left to right) The Duke and Duchess of York, Her Majesty Queen Elizabeth II, Prince Charles, The Princess of Wales (behind), Princess Margaret and Margaret's son, Viscount Linley.

(Left) The Queen Mother accepting posies and cards from members of the crowds who have come to wish her a happy birthday. (Above) waving to well-wishers before disappearing inside with gifts and cards.

EARLS OF STRATHMORE & KINGHORNE

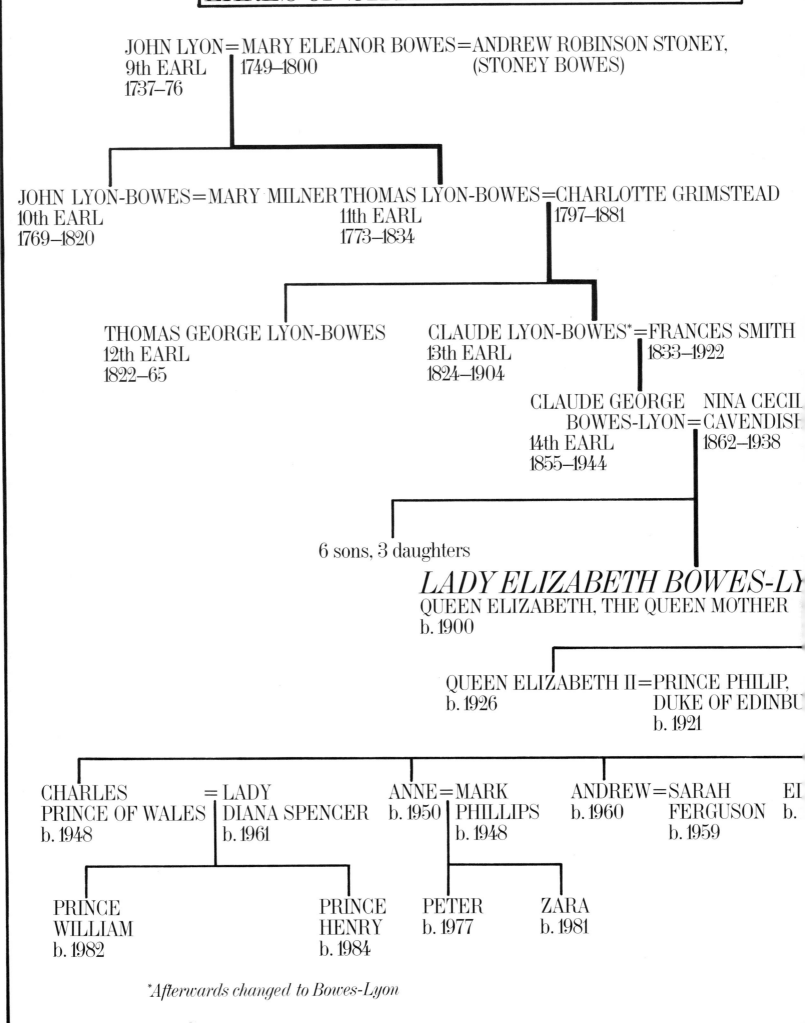

JOHN LYON=MARY ELEANOR BOWES=ANDREW ROBINSON STONEY,
9th EARL 1749–1800 (STONEY BOWES)
1737–76

JOHN LYON-BOWES=MARY MILNER THOMAS LYON-BOWES=CHARLOTTE GRIMSTEAD
10th EARL   11th EARL   1797–1881
1769–1820   1773–1834

THOMAS GEORGE LYON-BOWES   CLAUDE LYON-BOWES*=FRANCES SMITH
12th EARL   13th EARL   1833–1922
1822–65   1824–1904

CLAUDE GEORGE NINA CECIL
BOWES-LYON=CAVENDISH
14th EARL   1862–1938
1855–1944

6 sons, 3 daughters

LADY ELIZABETH BOWES-LY
QUEEN ELIZABETH, THE QUEEN MOTHER
b. 1900

QUEEN ELIZABETH II=PRINCE PHILIP,
b. 1926   DUKE OF EDINBU
                     b. 1921

CHARLES   =LADY   ANNE=MARK   ANDREW=SARAH   EI
PRINCE OF WALES DIANA SPENCER b. 1950 PHILLIPS b. 1960   FERGUSON   b.
b. 1948   b. 1961   b. 1948   b. 1959

PRINCE   PRINCE   PETER   ZARA
WILLIAM   HENRY   b. 1977 b. 1981
b. 1982   b. 1984

Afterwards changed to Bowes-Lyon

Family Tree of Queen Elizabeth
The Queen Mother

THE ROYAL FAMILY

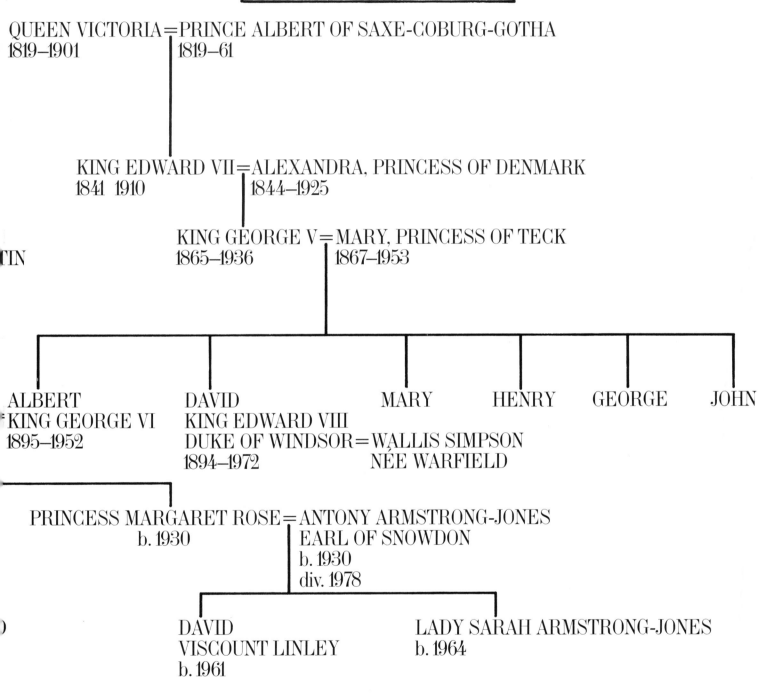

QUEEN VICTORIA=PRINCE ALBERT OF SAXE-COBURG-GOTHA
1819–1901   1819–61

KING EDWARD VII=ALEXANDRA, PRINCESS OF DENMARK
1841 1910   1844–1925

KING GEORGE V=MARY, PRINCESS OF TECK
1865–1936   1867–1953

TIN

ALBERT   DAVID   MARY   HENRY   GEORGE   JOHN
KING GEORGE VI   KING EDWARD VIII
1895–1952   DUKE OF WINDSOR=WALLIS SIMPSON
                    1894–1972   NÉE WARFIELD

PRINCESS MARGARET ROSE=ANTONY ARMSTRONG-JONES
         b. 1930   EARL OF SNOWDON
                            b. 1930
                            div. 1978

)

DAVID   LADY SARAH ARMSTRONG-JONES
VISCOUNT LINLEY   b. 1964
b. 1961